MW00638401

The Apostolic LIFE

The
Apostolic
LIFE

David K. Bernard

WORD AFLAME PRESS

The Apostolic Life

by David K. Bernard

Printed in United States of America

Printed by

WORD AFLAME PRESS
8855 Dunn Road, Hazelwood, MO 63042
www.pentecostalpublishing.com

Library of Congress Cataloging-in-Publication Data

Bernard, David K., 1956–
   The apostolic life : perspectives on christian living, doctrine, and ministry / David K. Bernard.
         p. cm.
   ISBN-13: 978-1-56722-695-9
      1. Theology, Doctrinal. 2. Oneness Pentecosstal churches—Doctrines. 3. Oneness doctrine (Pentecostalism) I. Title.
BT75.3.B47 2006
230'.994—dc22

                                                      2006020407

Other Books by David K. Bernard

Order from:
Pentecostal Publishing House
8855 Dunn Road
Hazelwood, MO 63042-2299
Tel:314.837.7300
Voicemail:314.837.7304 ext. 455
Fax:314.837.6574
Email:pphsales@upci.org
Web:PentecostalPublishing.com

Contents

Ministry

Outreach

Science and Scripture

Preface

The articles in this book cover many topics, but the common theme is a vision of what it means to be apostolic. They investigate how to apply apostolic identity to various aspects of life and ministry. Most were previously published in the *Pentecostal Herald* (official periodical of the United Pentecostal Church International), the *Forward* (periodical for UPCI ministers), or the *South Texas Vision* (official periodical of the South Texas District UPCI).

The articles are essentially the same as originally published. I made minor editorial changes to conform to current style and to address a more general audience. For instance, I deleted some references to particular audiences or events. I also inserted some clarifications and corrections.

Many of my previous books have discussed the major topics of Oneness Pentecostal theology. Thus, for the doctrinal section of this book, I chose articles that addressed specific points which I have not fully covered elsewhere and for which I have received requests.

In a few cases there is some overlap of content in articles written for different audiences, such as with "The Paradox of Preaching" and "The Paradox of the Cross." Rather than change either, I decided to leave both intact. One article, "Supernatural Spiritual Gifts," was adapted from one of my books, *Spiritual Gifts*, and is included because it seems to be a useful summary.

"The Charismatic Ministry of Women in the Early Church" is different in tone because it is a scholarly article written for a master's degree program at a secular university. As such, I approached the subject descriptively and interacted with a wide range of scholars, including some with whom I disagree strongly. I discussed biblical statements in a historical setting, but of course I strongly affirm the divine inspiration of Scripture. The word "charismatic" in the title refers to a gift of God's grace (from the Greek *charism*) as opposed to an institutional position.

The articles in the section entitled "Outreach" were written for the general public, without assuming that readers would be familiar with Scripture or accept its authority. I included them as examples of how to communicate the apostolic faith in our society. For those who purchase the book, limited permission is hereby granted to reprint one or more of these outreach articles in a local newspaper or church newsletter. This permission is granted on the condition that no one receive remuneration and that the following credit is given: "By David K. Bernard. Used by permission of Word Aflame Press."

Christian
LIVING

CHAPTER 1

An Apostolic Vision

And they continued stedfastly in the apostles' doctrine and fellowship, and in breaking of bread, and in prayers . . . praising God, and having favour with all the people. And the Lord added to the church daily such as should be saved (Acts 2:42, 47).

It is the will of God for the church to fulfill a threefold apostolic vision.

First, we must maintain our *apostolic identity*. We exist as a movement because we proclaim the beautiful, scriptural truths of the oneness of God in Jesus Christ, the new birth experience of Acts 2:38, the lifestyle of inward and outward holiness, heartfelt worship, and miracles and gifts of the Spirit. We must always treasure and champion this message. There is plenty of room for growth in grace and knowledge, but there is no room for compromise or abandonment of these fundamentals.

Second, we must have *apostolic unity*. We must unite in fellowship, in prayer, and in the common cause of winning the lost. While we have the right to different opinions

in matters of personal preferences and organizational decisions, all of us have the responsibility to reach out to one
another with mutual support, prayer, forgiveness, and love.
All of us need to be involved in the work of the kingdom of
God in and beyond our local church.

Third, we must have *apostolic revival*. When we continue steadfastly in apostolic identity and unity, then we
can expect miracles of healing, deliverance, and salvation.
Our heartbeat must be souls. We need a continual renewal
of the saints and a continual harvest of the lost. We must
seize this historic opportunity to grow existing churches,
to plant new churches and daughter works, and to evangelize the diverse population of our area, including
minorities such as Hispanics, African-Americans, and
Asian-Americans. Otherwise, we have no reason to exist.

In order to fulfill this apostolic vision, we need the active
involvement of men and women who are called of God. We
need ministers to work to fulfill the vision and to raise up lay
leaders as well as new ministers who have a call, burden,
and anointing. We must mobilize the whole church!

In addition, there are a number of qualified and
proven ministers among us who have not yet been
ordained. There is a special anointing that comes with
ordination, as the church and Holy Ghost jointly confirm
the call of God with the laying on of hands of the elders.
As these ministers are ordained, they will help launch the
church into a new dimension of revival and growth. It will
not be a formality but a spiritual breakthrough.

Together, let us make history as we fulfill the apostolic vision!

South Texas Vision, January-February 2003 (first issue)

CHAPTER 2

The Greatest Commandment

In the hustle and bustle of life, we need to keep our focus on things of ultimate priority. Recent events such as natural disasters remind us of what is truly valuable and what is transient and temporary. We must not become so busy tending to urgent things that we neglect the most important things.

What is most important? We find the answer in the following story, taken from Mark 12:28-31 (NIV):

> One of the teachers of the law came and heard them debating. Noticing that Jesus had given them a good answer, he asked him, "Of all the commandments, which is the most important?" "The most important one," answered Jesus, "is this: 'Hear, O Israel, the Lord our God, the Lord is one. Love the Lord your God with all your heart and with all your soul and with all your mind and with all your strength.' The second is this: 'Love your neighbor as yourself.' There is no commandment greater than these."

Our first priority is to worship the one true God with our whole being, including intellect, emotions, and will. When we do so, He will lead us into truth, reveal Himself to us, and supply our needs. If we do not, then we will succumb to sinfulness and deception, which ultimately lead to destruction.

Loving God means to establish and maintain a close personal relationship with Him. We do so through daily prayer and communion with Him, reading and meditating on His Word, entertaining His presence, faithfully participating in the life and worship of the church (which is His body), heeding the preaching and teaching of His Word, having fellowship with His people, walking by faith every day, being continually filled with His Spirit, and endeavoring to live a holy life according to His will.

Placing God first in our lives does not mean neglecting our family and society, for it is God's will that we establish and maintain strong, meaningful relationships with others and especially to fulfill our responsibilities to our families. If we truly love God, then we will love others also. God created humans in His image, so when we love Him we will love His image creatures.

Loving others includes treating them with kindness and respect, bearing their burdens, and ministering to their needs, both physical and spiritual. God desires humans to have fellowship with Him for eternity, to inherit eternal life rather than eternal death. Thus, both our love for God and our love for others will motivate us to fulfill God's plan by leading people into His kingdom. In other words, the greatest commandment leads directly to evangelism and discipleship.

Jesus came into this world to seek and to save the lost

(Luke 19:10). If we love Him, we will have the same desire. Indeed, Jesus left only one prayer request—that God would send laborers into the harvest (Luke 10:2). If we love Him, we will pray this prayer and also do our part to fulfill it.

When serving God is our top priority, God will bless all areas of our lives. Jesus promised, "Seek ye first the kingdom of God, and his righteousness; and all these things shall be added unto you" (Matthew 6:33).

New Life News, Austin, Texas, Winter 2006

CHAPTER 3

Loving One Another

Jesus said that a distinguishing mark of Christians would be the love they show toward each other. "By this shall all men know that ye are my disciples, if ye have love one to another" (John 13:35). How do we measure up to this standard?

In biblical terms, love is not primarily an emotion but a behavior. The focus is not on feelings but on action. For instance, Jesus taught us, "Love your enemies" (Matthew 5:44). This command does not require us to manufacture fond or romantic feelings toward those who mistreat us, but it teaches us to treat them kindly and compassionately, showing love in the face of persecution and opposition. Thus, Jesus went on to explain in the same verse, "Bless them that curse you, do good to them that hate you, and pray for them which despitefully use you, and persecute you."

James similarly explained that true Christian character is revealed not by what we profess but what we do: "If a brother or sister be naked, and destitute of daily food, and one of you say unto them, Depart in peace, be ye warmed and filled; notwithstanding ye give them not those things which are needful to the body; what doth it profit? Even so faith, if it hath not works, is dead, being alone" (James 2:15-17).

John also emphasized that we must express love by action. "Hereby perceive we the love of God, because he laid down his life for us: and we ought to lay down our lives for the brethren. But whoso hath this world's good, and seeth his brother have need, and shutteth up his bowels of compassion from him, how dwelleth the love of God in him? My little children, let us not love in word, neither in tongue; but in deed and in truth" (I John 3:16-18).

In fact, if we claim to love God but do not show love to people, then we only deceive ourselves. "If a man say, I love God, and hateth his brother, he is a liar: for he that loveth not his brother whom he hath seen, how can he love God whom he hath not seen? And this command-ment have we from him, That he who loveth God love his brother also" (I John 4:20-21).

As this passage indicates, love should begin within the church. Paul instructed, "As we have therefore oppor-tunity, let us do good unto all men, especially unto them who are of the household of faith" (Galatians 6:10). If we cannot act lovingly toward our fellow believers, then we certainly will not act lovingly toward unbelievers and opponents of truth.

Therefore, each of us needs to ask: Am I showing love toward others, especially fellow believers? Or more specifically: What am I doing to demonstrate and impart God's love to other people, especially those in the church?

Answering this question certainly includes the avoidance of any actions that could harm others. Thus we must not sow discord, cause strife, become talebearers, or put a stumbling block in people's lives. But answering this question also involves positive actions such as intercessory prayer, encouragement, courtesy, kindness, mercy, and practical forms of assistance in times of need.

Leaders should make a special effort to keep every minister and church informed and connected, to offer encouragement and fellowship, and to identify special needs to which our ministerial fellowship can respond. All ministers should stay connected and involved in the work of the fellowship and reach out to fellow ministers. If our brothers or sisters are in need, let us do what we can to encourage and support them.

Pastors, reach out to home missionaries and other pastors who need our encouragement and assistance. Be an inspiration, help them in times of financial need, and share their burden.

Saints, support the ministry of your pastor and church. Be a people helper and encourager, not a hindrance or weight to the church. Even if you are in a time of trial, don't focus on your own problems and needs, but find someone else who needs your friendship and support. Do not wait for others to minister to you, but minister to them.

One of the keys to revival and growth across our fellowship is for us to help one another and love one another. In doing so, we will show the world that we are truly Christians.

South Texas Vision, November-December 2004

CHAPTER 4

Apostolic Unity

In the church, one of the most important keys to success is unity. On the Day of Pentecost the believers "were all with one accord in one place" when the Holy Spirit fell on them (Acts 2:1). As people were added to the church, "they continued stedfastly in the apostles' doctrine and fellowship" (Acts 2:42).

When the church has unity, then it is able to grow. There can be differences of opinion at times, but we must not allow them to detract from our vision to proclaim the gospel of Jesus Christ in Spirit and truth.

Achieving and maintaining unity is not always easy, and we cannot take it for granted. Preventive maintenance is always in order. We must continue to work for unity, for disunity will hinder our growth and our spiritual success.

To maintain and increase unity, we must continue to pray for our fellowship, for leaders, for one another, and for people with whom we disagree. It is difficult to pray for someone and hold a grudge against them at the same time. Prayer is an effective means of helping us keep our focus and love one another.

Leaders must realize that God has given them a position in order to serve people, not lord it over them. (See Matthew 20:25-28.) Instead of being protective of their position or area of work, they should think foremost of what is best for the body and for fulfillment of the common vision. They should be open to suggestions from others and should always treat people with respect and consideration. They should be open to change, even if it involves their own responsibilities. All of us need to be flexible, ready to serve in the best way possible at the time, and ready to involve others. This advice is good for ministers at all levels of leadership (including the district superintendent and district board) as well as for lay leaders in the local church.

Followers—and we are all followers in some way or another—should cooperate with leaders and the direction that they give. If there is something with which you do not agree, you have several appropriate ways to respond, but grumbling, complaining, and sowing discord are not biblical options!

First, you can pray—talk to the Lord about the problem. This serves to resolve many issues. Second, if a problem still needs to be addressed, go to the person directly or else go to someone in leadership who has the authority and responsibility to deal with the matter. By offering your suggestions and recommendations with a right attitude, you may do much good. Third, once leadership has made a decision on the matter, be supportive and cooperative—or at least do nothing to harm or hinder!

Ministers need to understand the importance of ministerial ethics in preserving our unity. It is simply wrong to solicit people to switch from one apostolic church to another—whether the solicitation is direct and explicit or indirect and subtle. While there are sometimes legitimate reasons for people to go to a new church, such as a job transfer, we should encourage people to be faithful and loyal to their home church and to do everything possible to resolve any problems that may arise.

Moreover, if some indicate an intention to transfer, the pastor of the church they visit should advise them to counsel with their own pastor and, if there is a problem, to seek all possible means of reconciliation. Then he should contact their pastor to advise him of the situation. He should not offer to accept them as members or promise them positions.

At the same time, pastors should realize that if people are determined to find another church, it is probably best for all concerned to let them leave on peaceful terms, praying that another church can minister to them effectively and that God will deal with them in the areas of their need. Good communication between pastors and a joint plan of action can help stabilize many situations and often bring reconciliation and harmony.

In summary, unity means that at times we sacrifice our thoughts, feelings, and convenience for the good of the body. But in the long run, all of us benefit by belonging to one body that has the blessing of Almighty God. "Behold, how good and how pleasant it is for brethren to dwell together in unity! . . . For there the LORD commanded the blessing, even life for evermore" (Psalm 133:1, 3).

South Texas Vision, May-June 2004

CHAPTER 5

Unity of Spirit and Faith

Endeavouring to keep the unity of the Spirit in the bond of peace . . . till we all come in the unity of the faith (Ephesians 4:3, 13).

We shall endeavor to keep the unity of the Spirit until we all come into the unity of the faith, at the same time admonishing all brethren that they shall not contend for their different views to the disunity of the body (Fundamental Doctrine, UPCI, paragraph 2).

The Apostolic Pentecostal movement is greatly blessed of God, but sometimes people express concerns about our direction. Sometimes these concerns are based on inaccurate or partial information, but there are also important issues, such as how to respond to the teaching of erroneous and divisive doctrines. In such cases, there is the potential for serious confusion and division if the doctrines are not addressed directly. The body needs to pray for God to give direction to preserve doctrinal integrity and at the same time perpetuate revival around the world.

The handling of such matters gives us a good opportunity to review some biblical and ethical guidelines for dealing with differences that arise within the church.

- Doctrinal deviations are properly handled by thorough investigation followed by careful consideration and action by those in spiritual authority.
- Concerns about leadership are properly handled by personal dialogue, discussion in the governing body if necessary, and ultimately by the process specified in organizational documents.
- In neither case is it appropriate to resort to political campaigns or inflammatory rhetoric.
- In times of disagreement, we should focus our attention and deliberation on principles, rather than personalities, personal feelings, or personal hurts. We must always handle differences according to biblical ethics. Even Michael the archangel did not bring "a railing accusation" against the devil himself but simply said, "The Lord rebuke thee" (Jude 9).
- Holiness involves outward standards such as the way we use technology, but it also involves inward standards such as the way we use the tongue and pen and the way we treat other people, especially our spiritual leaders. This is true in the local church, and it is true in the international church.
- We should judge a matter carefully, obtaining full information and considering both sides. We should not be quick to believe hearsay reports, especially if they are detrimental to those who have a proven character and ministry among us.

28

- We owe courtesy and respect to each other as fellow Christians, especially to those who have labored faithfully in gospel work for many years and to those who have been chosen as leaders. We have the right to express our opinions, to disagree, and to vote, but always in humility and love.
- We all need to pray that God will help our movement to maintain biblical doctrine, holiness (inward and outward), brotherly love, ministerial ethics, and unity of faith and Spirit.

In situations such as these, may we never fall under the condemnation of Proverbs 6:16-19 in any way: "These six things doth the LORD hate: yea, seven are an abomination unto him: a proud look, a lying tongue, and hands that shed innocent blood, an heart that deviseth wicked imaginations, feet that be swift in running to mischief, a false witness that speaketh lies, and he that soweth discord among brethren." Rather, let us fulfill Colossians 3:14-15: "And above all these things put on charity, which is the bond of perfectness. And let the peace of God rule in your hearts, to the which also ye are called in one body; and be ye thankful."

South Texas Vision, November-December 2003

CHAPTER 6

A Thirst for More

Blessed are they which do hunger and thirst after righteousness: for they shall be filled (Matthew 5:6).

While we rightly rejoice over the blessings of God and the progress of the church, we cannot afford to become complacent. We are still laying a foundation for a great future, should the Lord tarry. We are at the threshold of the kind of revival that God wants to give us. We have only just begun to see what God desires to do in our midst.

Therefore, we must have what I call "holy dissatisfaction." While we should be thankful for what God has already done, we should not be satisfied with the results we have seen, but we must thirst for more. A sense of urgency and even desperation must grip us. The harvest is great, the laborers are few, and time is short! In these last days, God wants to pour out His Spirit upon all flesh—and most of the world has never heard the full gospel message, much less experienced it.

The good news is that Jesus has promised to fill all who would hunger and thirst for righteousness. This principle applies to those who are seeking salvation, and it also applies to those who are seeking an outpouring of the Holy Spirit for their churches and communities.

When people are truly thirsty, their need for water supersedes anything else. Finding water becomes their utmost priority. Nothing else matters. It does not matter if the water is warm or cool, clean or dirty; they are looking for something wet to slake their thirst.

As a child, I remember staying in Mokpo, Korea, with my missionary parents as they held a revival there. The city was suffering a drought during a hot summer. There was no city water, and even the wells had run dry. Vendors would fill old wine bottles with water and haul them into the city on carts as soon as the dawn curfew lifted. By early morning the water would be sold out for the day.

At night, after exuberant worship and prayer in a hot, crowded building with no air conditioning, my sister and I wanted as much water as we could have. Just before bedtime, we would beg our father for water, but none would be left. It was hard for us to go to sleep while we were thirsty. We would make Dad promise that as soon as he purchased water in the morning he would wake us up and give us a drink, no matter how early it was.

The next morning when we awoke, we would ask for water. He would explain that he had already awakened us and had given us our drink for the morning, just as he had promised. But we were still thirsty. We would protest that we didn't remember waking up and getting a drink. We wanted more.

That experience taught me how powerful thirst can

be and how desperate we can become when we are truly thirsty. In the same way, the Lord wants us to be thirsty for His presence and the outpouring of His Spirit.

Let us pray fervently for a mighty revival in our churches and across our fellowship. A spirit of revival will help us overcome any internal problems as we focus on winning souls, discipling converts, and growing the church. As someone has said, if we do not have revival, nothing else matters. And if we do have revival, nothing else matters.

South Texas Vision, January-February 2005

CHAPTER 7

Saved by Truth

The most destructive tsunami in human history hit Asia on December 26, 2004. On February 19, the Reuters news service estimated that this violent wall of water killed up to 300,000 people. We were all saddened by this tragedy, but I would like to focus on two amazing stories of deliverance as reported by Yahoo! News on January 2, 2005.

The headline of the first story was "Elders' Sea Knowledge Spares Some Thais," and it told about a group of Thai fisherman known as the Morgan sea gypsies. Although they had never seen a tsunami, the knowledge of the ocean and its currents as passed down from generation to generation saved their entire village. The sixty-five-year-old village chief, Sarma Kathalay, explained, "The elders told us that if the water recedes fast it will reappear in the same quantity in which it disappeared."

The first sign of an impending tsunami is when the sea drains out of the beaches. When that happened in Thailand in December 2004, many people headed to the beach to see this unusual sight and to pick up fish left flopping on the sand. They had no idea that the receding water was a warning of tragedy to come. Although the gypsies had never seen this sight either, they remembered the admonition of previous generations and headed for the hills. While others unknowingly hastened toward destruction, the gypsies hastened toward salvation. Why? They knew the truth about what was happening. And how did they know the truth when almost everyone else did not? Because the elders had faithfully preserved and transmitted the message, and the current generation believed and obeyed.

The second story was "British 'Angel' Saved Hundreds from Tsunami with Classroom Knowledge." It described a ten-year-old girl from Surrey in northern England who was on vacation in Phuket, Thailand, when the tsunami came. A few days earlier, she had learned about tsunamis in her geography class. The teacher had explained to the class that there are about ten minutes from the time the ocean draws out until the tsunami strikes.

The girl was on Maikhao Beach when she saw the water recede, and instantly she realized that a tsunami was coming. She raised an alarm, which prompted the evacuation of the beach and a neighboring hotel. As a result, she saved hundreds of lives.

Other beaches and hotels suffered heavy loss of life, but this beach and hotel were spared because of one schoolgirl. The people were saved because in a faraway classroom a teacher provided vital information, because a young girl learned that information and acted upon it, and because they believed the report of the young girl.

The spiritual lessons from these accounts are clear. First of all, if we want to be saved and to save others, we must have sufficient knowledge, and that knowledge must be according to the truth. God said, "My people are destroyed for lack of knowledge" (Hosea 4:6). But God desires for everyone "to be saved and to come to the knowledge of the truth" (I Timothy 2:4).

Second, like the elders of the sea gypsies and like the teacher in England, we must transmit truth. We must preserve and proclaim the gospel of Jesus Christ without compromise.

Finally, we must believe and obey truth. It is not enough to know truth; we must act upon it. Many people could have discounted the warning of the sea gypsies because it went beyond their knowledge, and many could have discounted the warning of the schoolgirl because of her youth and inexperience. But those who acted on the warning were saved.

We will not be saved merely because we grew up in a Pentecostal family or attended a Pentecostal church. We must develop a love for the truth that will cause us to embrace it and obey it despite doubts, objections, and opposition—perhaps even from others who claim to have truth. In the end time, deception and judgment will come upon people "because they did not receive the love of the truth, that they might be saved" (II Thessalonians 2:10).

Paul wrote, "Take heed to yourself and to the doctrine. Continue in them, for in doing this you will save both yourself and those who hear you" (I Timothy 4:16, NKJV). Let us hold fast to the apostolic experience, message, and lifestyle. In doing so, we will participate in the salvation that God has graciously provided, and we will also lead many other people to a saving relationship with Him.

South Texas Vision, March-April 2005

CHAPTER 8

Spiritual Warfare

The Bible compares the Christian life to a battle against the forces of evil. Like soldiers, we must be strong, courageous, disciplined, and properly equipped in order to win this war. "Finally, my brethren, be strong in the Lord, and in the power of his might. Put on the whole armour of God, that ye may be able to stand against the wiles of the devil" (Ephesians 6:10-11).

If we are to succeed in the Christian life, we must understand the nature of our warfare. We must discard some faulty concepts associated with earthly warfare and replace them with spiritual concepts.

First, our enemies are not other people, but the devil, the world, and the flesh. "For we wrestle not against flesh and blood, but against principalities, against powers, against the rulers of the darkness of this world, against spiritual wickedness in high places" (Ephesians 6:12).

This verse speaks of spiritual enemies—the devil, his evil angels (the demons), and human power structures that are under his influence and control. The devil is the enemy of God. Indeed, his name—Satan—means "adversary" in Hebrew. Since God created us in His image and for His glory, Satan is also our adversary, and he seeks to destroy us (I Peter 5:8).

Because of the devil's success in tempting Adam and Eve to sin in the Garden of Eden, the whole human race has fallen under the dominion of sin and is subject to the devil's evil influence. Satan has been able to dominate this world to such an extent that a "friend of the world is the enemy of God," and if someone loves the world then "the love of the Father is not in him" (James 4:4; I John 2:15). In this context, "world" does not refer to people but to the value system, the cultural mores, and the social structures of sinful humanity—specifically, the lust of the flesh, the lust of the eyes, and the pride of life (I John 2:16).

These terms point to an inward struggle as well. Not only are we tempted by the devil and by the sinful world around us, but we are assailed by sinful tendencies and desires stemming from our own fallen nature, which the Bible sometimes calls the "flesh." This "carnal mind" is the enemy of God (Romans 8:7). As children of God we have a new identity of holiness, but we still have the old desires for sin resident within us, and the two are in conflict. By the power of the indwelling Holy Spirit, we can overcome the desires of the flesh and pursue a victorious, godly life. (See Galatians 5:16-25.)

When people of the world oppose the church, or even when people in the church rise up against the work of God, we must remember that they are not our enemies. We cannot retaliate against them as if they were. Instead, we must recognize that they have been deceived by the devil, and knowingly or unknowingly, they are tools in his hands. Even as we oppose their evil actions, we must show love and compassion toward them, praying and working for their deliverance. "The servant of the Lord must not strive; but be gentle unto all men, apt to teach, patient, in meekness instructing those that oppose themselves; if God peradventure will give them repentance to the acknowledging of the truth; and that they may recover themselves out of the snare of the devil, who are taken captive by him at his will" (II Timothy 2:24-26).

Second, our warfare and its weapons are not physical but spiritual. "For though we walk in the flesh, we do not war after the flesh: (for the weapons of our warfare are not carnal, but mighty through God to the pulling down of strong holds;) casting down imaginations, and every high thing that exalteth itself against the knowledge of God, and bringing into captivity every thought to the obedience of Christ" (II Corinthians 10:3-5).

This passage emphasizes that we cannot expect to win our spiritual battle with weapons of the flesh. It is obvious that swords, guns, and even nuclear weapons cannot destroy sin. We cannot expect any earthly war to vanquish evil in our world or in our lives. Instead, the only hope for the world is a spiritual battle to change the hearts and lives of people. As the church, our commission is to wage spiritual warfare by preaching the whole gospel to the whole world, converting souls, and making them disciples of Jesus Christ.

Nor can the tactics of the world and the flesh enable us to defeat our adversaries. For example, "the wrath of man worketh not the righteousness of God" (James 1:20). Sometimes we are tempted to implement our understanding of God's will by carnal means of manipulation, threat, slander, political maneuvering, authoritarianism, legalism, and so on. Or we may think that the key to revival lies in showmanship, entertainment, and "enticing words of man's wisdom" (I Corinthians 2:4). But these methods will never produce the righteousness of God. Instead, we must rely on the Word of God, the Spirit of God, and the power of love to overcome all obstacles so that we can accomplish God's purpose and inspire others to believe and obey Christ.

Spiritual warfare consists of pulling down spiritual strongholds—fortresses in the mind and spirit. We must battle against "imaginations" (thoughts, arguments, reasoning) and "every high thing" (pretension, barrier) that sets itself up against the knowledge of God. We must "take captive every thought to make it obedient to Christ" (NIV).

In other words, the true battleground is the human heart. We must conquer pride, rebellion, lust, and other evil attitudes within our own hearts and impose the spiritual discipline of the Word of God. We must open our lives to the work of the Holy Spirit to transform us into the likeness of Christ.

Here is a partial statement of the methods and goals of this battle: "Walk worthy of the vocation wherewith ye are called, with all lowliness and meekness, with longsuffering, forbearing one another in love; endeavouring to keep the unity of the Spirit in the bond of peace. . . . Let all bitterness, and wrath, and anger, and clamour, and evil speaking, be put away from you, with all malice: and be ye kind one to another, tenderhearted, forgiving one another, even as God for Christ's sake hath forgiven you" (Ephesians 4:1-3, 31-32).

As an example, when Paul urged the Corinthian church to show forgiveness toward a sinning member who had repented, he gave this reason: "lest Satan should get an advantage of us: for we are not ignorant of his devices" (II Corinthians 2:11). In other words, an unforgiving spirit opens the door for Satan to attack us. It could become a stronghold of evil in our minds—and in our fellowship—that would block us from receiving the victory that God has planned for us.

Third, we cannot earn victory by our ability, but we must recognize that Jesus Christ has already won the victory at Calvary and apply His victory to our lives. When Jesus died on the cross, He paid the price for our sins and satisfied the just requirements of God's holy law. When Jesus rose from the dead, He won victory over sin, death, and the devil. If we believe on Him and obey His gospel, we share in that victory. Jesus Christ came in human flesh so that "through death he might destroy him that had the power of death, that is, the devil; and deliver them who through fear of death were all their lifetime subject to bondage" (Hebrews 2:14-15).

When one of its generals won a significant battle, Rome would conduct a great victory procession called a triumph. The general would strip his defeated foes of their regalia and arms and parade them through the streets of the city, bound and humiliated. At the climax of the celebration, the victor would put his foot on the head of the defeated leader as he bowed to the ground. All the people could see that the enemies they had feared were reduced to helpless captives.

That is what God did in Christ, when He made provision for our sins on the cross and defeated Satan's schemes against us: "When you were dead in your sins and in the uncircumcision of your sinful nature, God made you alive with Christ. He forgave us all our sins, having canceled the written code, with its regulations, that was against us and that stood opposed to us; he took it away, nailing it to the cross. And having disarmed the powers and authorities, he made a public spectacle of them, triumphing over them by the cross" (Colossians 2:13-15, NIV).

Thus, for the Christian, Satan has already been defeated. He has no grounds to condemn the child of God, and he has no power to force the child of God to do anything. For this reason, James 4:7 instructs, "Submit yourselves therefore to God. Resist the devil, and he will flee from you."

Satan can still tempt us as long as we are in this life. If we listen to him, he still has the ability to deceive us. He can attack and even oppress us for a time, but he cannot possess or destroy us, for "greater is he that is in you, than he that is in the world" (I John 4:4). Therefore, we need not fear him. We must be aware of him and his tactics, but we need not be preoccupied with him. He can bluff us with a frightening roar, but when we call his bluff in the name of Jesus, he can do nothing more against us.

In short, we do not need to focus on various formulas, strategies, or techniques of spiritual warfare in an attempt to outmaneuver the devil. In any case, we cannot defeat him by our own abilities and actions. Instead, we must apply the victory that Christ has already won for us by His blood. Thus, Ephesians 6:14-18 counsels us to put on the spiritual armor of truth, righteousness, the gospel of peace, faith, salvation, and the Word of God, and to be fervent in prayer. These are the weapons by which we apply Christ's victory to our lives, call Satan's bluff, and defeat his tactics.

While we recognize that Satan has powerful forces at his command, the key to victory does not lie in our having an extensive knowledge of those forces. Rather, as we draw close to God in prayer, trust in Him, and consecrate ourselves to His service, He sets in motion what is necessary to thwart the devil's efforts. Daniel prayed but did not receive an immediate answer because of supernatural opposition from "the prince of the kingdom of Persia." How did Daniel prevail against this formidable spiritual opposition? God sent an angelic messenger to answer Daniel's prayer and also dispatched the archangel Michael to defeat the prince of Persia. Daniel was not even aware of the exact nature of the opposition, and he was not able to develop a special strategy in response, but he simply continued to pray, trust God, and live a consecrated life until the answer came. (See Daniel 10:12-14.)

Likewise, the apostles faced much spiritual opposition as they carried the gospel throughout the ancient world and established the New Testament church. They did not have detailed strategies to counter the various attacks and emissaries of the devil, but they successfully accomplished their mission by preaching the gospel, teaching the truth, praising God in all things, praying consistently and fervently in the name of Jesus, working in unity, and walking in the Spirit with miraculous power. (See Acts 2:42-47; 4:24-33.)

Finally, to be victorious we must stand firm in the faith and pray continually in the Spirit. The great scriptural passage on spiritual warfare and spiritual armor, Ephesians 6:10-17, admonishes us to "be strong in the Lord," "to stand against the wiles of the devil," "to withstand in the evil day," and "having done all, to stand."

Here we see the importance of determination, commitment, and personal convictions. In the final analysis, no one can fight in our stead. We must stand firm on the victory that Christ has won for us. We must take a personal stand on doctrinal truth, holiness of life, and personal consecrations. Then having done all—continue to stand.

We do not stand in our own ability, however. At the end of the discussion of spiritual warfare, we read: "And pray in the Spirit on all occasions with all kinds of prayers and requests. With this in mind, be alert and always keep on praying for all the saints" (Ephesians 6:18, NIV). We are victorious only as long as we depend upon the saving work of Jesus Christ—only as long as we trust in Him, plead His blood, call upon His name, follow His Word, and rely upon the power of His Spirit. As we stand we must continue to pray and be yielded to the Holy Spirit. By God's grace, we will win the victory!

Pentecostal Herald, October 2004

CHAPTER 9

Finding God's Will in Life

What am I going to do with my life? This is a question that all of us face at one time or another. In answering this question, it is necessary to find the will of God, but many people are confused as to how to do so. Let us look at how the will of God works in our lives.

God's Will Is Not Mystical

First of all, the will of God is not mystical. It is not a magical revelation that brings an instantaneous answer to all of life's decisions. I have found that God's will is most clearly revealed by gentle leadings and alterations in direction while I am already doing His will. God has given us intelligence and He has given us His Word; He expects us to use both. The will of God has never come to me as I stand by idly. I do not mean to discount the value of supernatural experiences in which God speaks by a dream, an angel, or an audible voice. However, these are exceptional manifestations for exceptional circumstances. We should not wait around for this type of guidance to the point that we ignore the many other less dramatic ways God has of leading us in our everyday lives. When such a revelation does occur, it usually follows a long period in which the person involved has already been seeking and doing the will of God.

Doing What We Know to Do

By far, the greatest part of finding the will of God consists in simply doing what we already know to do. Much of the will of God has already been revealed to us by the Bible and by spiritual leaders who teach and apply the Bible. For example, if we want God's will in marriage, we should start by dating apostolic Christians. If we want to do a work for God, we should start by winning souls in our community. If we feel a call to work in the church, we should start by doing whatever we find to do, whether it means teaching Sunday school or sweeping the church building. If we desire a closer walk with God, then we should develop a system of personal devotion and Bible study.

If we are unwilling to do the little things that we know to be God's will, why should we expect God to reveal greater things? If we have not established a solid personal relationship with Jesus Christ, why should we expect Him to communicate His will to us? If we are not involved in soulwinning efforts where we are, why should we expect God to call us to any other type of ministry?

The will of God is an evolving process. If we will do everything we know to do and if we will keep God first in our lives, then God will direct our steps. (See Proverbs 3:5-7; Matthew 6:33; Romans 8:28.)

Often we want God to reveal in an instant His plan for our entire lives. If He did, however, most of us would not be able to grasp, understand, or accept it. I have found that God only reveals enough of His will for me to take the next step along the way. If I am doing what I know to do now, God will give direction for the future when the time comes to make those decisions.

The Open Door Policy

There is no use worrying about decisions that are in the future. We should prepare for those decisions, but we must trust in God to help us make the right decisions at the right time.

I follow what I call the Open Door Policy. When I see a major decision down the road, I try to think of all alternatives. I let my mind go free and think of all kinds of possibilities that I ordinarily would not consider. This approach prevents me from getting in a rut, from being too narrow-minded, or from being influenced too much by the people and circumstances that surround me at the moment. It opens me up in the event God has something for me that is far different from my previous experience and thought.

After I have made this mental or written list of alternatives, I start eliminating those I can through prayer, thought, and discussion. Even so, there are usually several good options left. Then, I ask God to eliminate all options but the right one by the time the decision must be made. I ask Him to open the right doors and close the other doors. I ask Him to influence events so that everything will fall into place for the right choice and to influence my mind so that I will be excited about and satisfied with that result.

In the meantime, I try to keep all options open as

long as possible and to walk through every door that God opens. My goal is to plan for the future, yet give God the opportunity to change and influence my plans. Moreover, I want to do whatever I can for God now, while He is working out the larger plan for my life.

In following this approach, I usually commit myself to one year at a time. Of course, I have plans, visions, and dreams for the future, but I recognize that they can change or develop in unforeseen ways. If I plan too rigidly, I will not leave God enough room to operate. On the other hand, if I do not make definite plans and establish certain goals, then I will never accomplish anything.

My Experience

Let me give some examples from my own life. When I came to the United States at age seventeen, my goal was to get a four-year college degree from Rice University in Houston, Texas. A lot of things can happen in four years, so I realized that this plan was subject to change. However, I definitely planned to finish the first year. My mind was already settled that I was in the will of God. I did not have to reevaluate this decision every month; no matter what happened, I was determined to finish that year of school.

As each school year ended, I evaluated my life spiritually, mentally, and emotionally and decided that nothing had intervened to change my basic plan. However, I did change majors, added a second major, and changed certain career goals during this period as various decision times came. It would have been foolish to make unalterable decisions about classes, major, and career in my first semester, or to try to force God to reveal them to me in that time. Rather, I had a basic plan that could and did change as I learned more about myself and about possible careers. I gave God time to direct and influence my choices.

During this time, I tried to put God first in all my activities. I decided that if I would put Him first and college second, then He would bless both my spiritual life and my college work. I promised God that I would walk through any door He opened as far as service for Him was concerned. As a result I became involved in Sunday school, youth work, bus ministry, visitation, campus ministry, and so on.

God helped me to work my way through college, be active in church, and finish my courses satisfactorily. True, I did not have time to participate in many of the college's extracurricular activities, but I had something far more important: I had kept my salvation and I had done God's will and work to the best of my ability. As a result I had confidence that He would direct my next step. And He did!

Next, I entered the University of Texas School of Law in Austin. Again I made the same commitment to God— to put Him first and to walk through whatever doors of service He opened. Once again I became involved in all the activities mentioned before and more. Soon I was asked to teach Bibles studies, to speak in various services, and then to speak in neighboring churches. I did not actively seek any of these opportunities but simply asked God to open doors. At each step, I prayed, checked with my pastor, and then went ahead. God blessed my efforts and continued to open doors. Without any dramatic revelation, God led me further into His will and into His plan.

My last summer of law school, I went to Beaumont, Texas, to work for a law firm. Even though I did not know anyone in Beaumont and did not advertise myself as a speaker or preacher, I had the opportunity to teach or preach twenty-one times in eleven weeks.

By the end of the summer, I knew God was calling me into the full-time preaching ministry. I finished law school that year but turned down all job opportunities and interviews. I was confident that God would show me the next step in His own time. Sure enough, two weeks before my graduation and five weeks before my marriage, God opened the door for me to teach full time in Bible college.

Let me emphasize again that we should concentrate on doing all that we already know to do. Instead of just waiting around for God to dump His will on us, we must get busy doing what we find to do and trust Him to direct us in the process. If we are moving, God will steer us and possibly change our direction, but if we are standing still, we will not go anywhere.

Conclusion

In summary, here are some recommendations for staying in the will of God:

First of all, pray. I depend heavily on James 1:5-7, which gives us the right to pray for wisdom.

Second, be consistent and focused—in personal devotion, relationships, God's work, secular work, and achieving of goals.

Third, seek advice and guidance. God uses pastors and parents (even unsaved parents) to give us direction. I like to get a variety of opinions from friends, acquaintances, and elders even though I do not follow every recommendation. Exposure to advice from others can open new avenues of thought, and the cumulative effect of advice often points decisively in a certain direction. (See Proverbs 11:14; 20:5.)

Fourth, always put God first. We must be determined to live for Him and do His will regardless of the cost, obey His Word in all things, be willing to lay aside plans, dreams, and opportunities if they conflict with God's plan, be open to new directions, and put God first in the budgeting of time and money.

Fifth, use the Open Door Policy—consider various options, eliminate those you can, ask God to eliminate others, ask God to open the right doors, and then walk through those doors.

Finally, be patient until the time for decision actually comes, yet be ready to respond to God at any time.

Conqueror, May 1988

CHAPTER 10

Career Planning and God's Will

How should a Christian go about choosing a job or a career? How can he or she know God's will for this very important area of life? In discussing the subject, we need to understand some important concepts about Christians and careers.

Careers and Christian Service

First, every Christian has a personal ministry. (See Romans 12:4-8.) Every one of us is called to be a witness and to do a work for God. Our careers are important avenues of ministry.

We need to discard the idea that the professional ministry is the only group of Christians called to work for God. All of us are called to work for God. All of us are called to win souls and to minister (help, serve) to those around us. Each believer can be as much in the will of God, as close to God, and as much a part of His plan in a secular career as those in the professional ministry. In fact, the church needs intelligent, capable people in careers where they can reach people and perform functions that a preacher cannot.

We also need to get rid of the idea that part of our lives can be categorized as secular and part as spiritual. Every aspect of our lives should be permeated with the spiritual. We can and should serve God in our careers and in our daily lives. In this way we can be witnesses to everyone. (See Matthew 5:13-16; II Corinthians 3:2-3; I Thessalonians 4:11-12.)

Second, we need to reach everyone with the gospel. The church must be able to minister at all levels of society. This means we need people in a variety of careers and from a cross section of society. We need people who can relate to the rich as well as the poor, the educated as well as the uneducated, the professional as well as the unskilled laborer.

Too often in the past we have shunned education and the professions in the mistaken belief that our God was too weak to protect us from the threats of skepticism, agnosticism, and materialism. A number of prominent people in the Bible rose to high levels in their ungodly societies and yet maintained integrity. Joseph, Daniel, Shadrach, Meshach, Abednego, and Esther are good examples. Luke was a physician, and Paul was one of the most educated and cultured men of his day. All of the apostles were great, but it was Paul whom God sent to represent the gospel before philosophers in Athens, governors, kings, and ultimately the Roman emperor himself.

I firmly believe and have seen in my own experience that a Pentecostal young person can successfully attend a university while maintaining and increasing his or her faith. Here are the keys to spiritual success in this area: (1) Come with firmly established beliefs and a solid experience with God. (2) Put God and church activities ahead of school. (3) Do not accept everything that you hear, but use what you can and learn all you can about how other people think. (4) Make living arrangements that are conducive to your spiritual life. I decided that I could best maintain my spiritual balance by not living on campus.

Christians can also enter businesses and professions and still live for God by following these principles. However, they must always remain willing to drop a job or career if it conflicts with God's will or becomes detrimental to spiritual growth.

Christians should consider their jobs or careers as avenues of ministry. Through them they can influence people whom no one else will ever reach. Here are some tips for soulwinning on the job: (1) Witnessing by example, by bearing fruit of the Spirit (Galatians 5:22-23), is the most important and effective way to witness. (2) Attitudes are very important. We must avoid being obnoxious, self-righteous, argumentative, or abrasive. (3) Friendship is the best way to win a soul. The way to be a friend is to be helpful at all times, to listen to others, to pray for them, and to give counsel and prayer when they seek help. (4) Personal testimonies and invitations to church are also important but should be given in a receptive atmosphere and then only when preceded by the first three things.

A Time of Preparation

It is also important to realize that every life has a period of transition and preparation. In our day, few of us are ready to embark upon our life's career or find our ultimate place in God's plan as soon as we get out of high school. The first reaction of many at this time is to get

57

married or to immediately attempt a dramatic work for God. However, few are ready to be so successful so soon. Those who achieve early success typically rely heavily on extra help from others and could be even more successful if they would invest more time in preparation. We need to give God time to work His will in our lives, and we need to give ourselves time to prepare for whatever God has for us.

Here are some goals to seek during the transition between the teenage years and the time of settling down with family, career, home, long-term goals, and more definite direction from God: (1) gaining experience and learning useful skills, (2) learning discipline and responsibility, (3) developing interpersonal skills and personal relationships, (4) developing self-confidence and self-reliance, (5) saving money and investing wisely, (6) developing versatility, (7) being exposed to new persons, experiences, and ideas, and (8) developing a strong personal relationship and communication with Jesus Christ. Before people jump headlong into a career, a marriage, or a ministry, they would do well to get a good start on these goals.

Here are some ways to spend this period of transition and preparation: secular college, Bible college, vocational school, non-career jobs, and travel. College is not for everyone, but it ought to be considered more than it is. The value of any type of college is not just in book learning but in the achieving of many of the preceding goals.

Whether considering further education or a job, analyze how your choice will help you achieve the listed goals. If you get a job, get one that will teach you a useful skill or how to work with people. Then work your way into a position of responsibility and stick with it until you make more definite career plans. If you change jobs, make the kind of change that will help you achieve these goals; do not change merely out of boredom or uncertainty.

Especially while you are single, consider the option of travel—as a tourist, to a conference, on a missions trip, or as an Associate In Missions.

Finally, during this time of transition get involved in a church, because this will set patterns for life and will help you to find the areas in which you can best minister. Possibilities are visitation, Sunday school, bus ministry, music, institutional ministries, deaf ministry, youth work, home Bible studies, and other forms of outreach.

Choosing a Career

Now let us discuss the specifics of choosing a career. A career should provide three things: (1) the opportunity to be in the will of God and work for Him, (2) satisfaction and enjoyment, and (3) a living.

The first step in finding the right career for you is to *evaluate yourself.* What are your *interests*—your likes and dislikes? What are your *aptitudes*—your skills and abilities? High school and college counselors have tests that can aid in this evaluation. One type of test is the vocational interest test, which asks a wide range of questions and compares your answers to those of people in different careers. This test gives you a good idea of how your interests compare with those of people who are happy in certain careers. Aptitude tests tell you where your strong and weak points are.

59

To help in self-evaluation, here is a list of some important abilities. In parentheses are examples of careers in which each ability is especially important. Many careers require strength in several of these areas.

1. Verbal or communicative (teacher)
2. Numerical (accountant)
3. Social (personnel manager)
4. Creative or artistic (artist)
5. Clerical (bank clerk)
6. Mechanical (machinist)
7. Abstract or logical (computer programmer)
8. Spatial (architect)
9. Musical (musician)
10. Selling (salesman)

In addition to evaluating your interests and abilities, you need to look at your *priorities*. How important are family ties, the local church, leisure time, geographical location, and material benefits?

The second step in choosing a career is to *evaluate potential jobs and careers*. What skills are required? What education and training are required? What is the nature of the work itself? What about location, and what is the likelihood that you will need to move to another location at some time? What is the compensation in terms of wages, salaries, and fringe benefits? What are the time requirements? What is the potential for advancement?

These questions will be of varying importance depending on your priorities. For example, if you do not have a strong preference for a particular city, your options are much greater. If you want to work a straight forty-hour week, you probably should not consider a professional career or go into business for yourself. If money is very important to you then this might eliminate a lower paying but otherwise satisfying career. If you really desire to advance to a high management position, this may eliminate some very small companies and some very large ones.

In actually making your choice, get counsel and advice from parents, friends, educators, and employers. They can often see things about you that are not immediately apparent to you, and they can give you needed confirmation.

Work experience can also give you valuable information. It is helpful to get some type of exposure to the actual work before making a final decision.

Finally, do not forget the spiritual considerations. What is your potential for ministering in this career? This could mean working full time for the church (music, education), using valuable skills to benefit the church (accounting, music, law, construction), or simply being strategically placed in the world to reach certain groups of people for God. Moreover, are there any potential conflicts with Christian living? This could be in the nature of the work, in the hours you work, in the geographical location, or even in the compensation. Your pastor can help you in these spiritual considerations.

My Experience

Let me share some examples from my own life. I enjoy teaching very much, but while in college I decided against a career in teaching because of the surplus of teachers at the time and the difficulty in getting a position that paid well by professional standards. Instead I chose law—a career that required many of the same skills but offered greater opportunities.

The choice did not come overnight. When I first entered college, law was in the back of my mind as a far-fetched idea. I was interested in liberal arts but decided not to major in any of them because of the lack of good job opportunities. Instead I majored in mathematical sciences and in managerial studies. However, after working with computers for a while and after working in accounting part time for three years, I decided that while I had the aptitude to work in either field and enjoyed both to some degree, I did not want to spend the rest of my life in either one.

After taking a vocational interest test, I was surprised to discover that my score was very high in the area of law. My score was also high in an aptitude test in law (the LSAT). I applied to some law schools and was accepted. I prayed about my decision over a period of months and talked to my pastor, my parents, and other spiritual leaders whom I respected about the spiritual aspects of my decision. I also consulted friends, college counselors, and college teachers. By the time I graduated from college I had my answer and enrolled in law school that fall. During this process I made two decisions about law as a career: (1) I would not enter the area of criminal law because I felt that the moral and spiritual tensions would be too great. (2) I would conduct my career on Christian principles, and if I could not, I would abandon that career.

During law school the Lord began dealing with me in another way. By the time I finished law school, I knew that He was calling me to the preaching ministry. But I do not believe that the years of secular education and work experience were in vain. They were in God's plan to prepare me for future ministry.

Conclusion

Career planning involves self-evaluation, career evaluation, a matching of the two, and an analysis of how our contribution to the work of God will be helped or hindered by the career we choose.

Set your goals and set them high. Don't be afraid to try new things or to seek a path different from what others are choosing. Be patient, but establish goals during your time of transition and preparation. Put God first and do everything that He has revealed to be His will for you. Look for the opportunity to make your job and career an avenue of ministry and an asset to the church. Trust in the Lord to direct you and to shape your life as you live for Him.

Conqueror, June 1988

CHAPTER 11

Apostolic Education

What role should education play in the Apostolic movement? On the one hand, we are living in an age of specialization in which various forms of training are beneficial or even necessary for certain careers. Moreover, in an increasingly diverse and complex society, it is helpful for people to obtain a variety of learning experiences that can enrich their lives and prepare them for future opportunities and challenges. On the other hand, secular education can undermine people's belief in the Bible.

What role should education play in the training of believers for Christian service—as pastors, teachers, and lay leaders? On the one hand, a Bible-based education can provide helpful tools for ministry. On the other hand, we cannot accomplish effective ministry simply by acquiring human knowledge and ability; we must have the power of the Holy Spirit.

The answer is that we need a variety of educational opportunities and experiences in the kingdom of God, but our supreme resources for Christian life and ministry must be the Word of God and the Spirit of God. Some people in the church will not need to pursue higher education, while others will obtain vocational or liberal arts training, a professional degree, or a theological education.

God uses ministers in different ways, according to His purpose, including those with little education and those with great education. The Galilean apostles were considered "ignorant and unlearned" by the religious elite in Jerusalem (Acts 4:13), yet they powerfully established the New Testament church upon the rock of Christ Jesus. At the same time, the apostle Paul had the ancient equivalent of a graduate degree in theology, and God used him mightily to establish churches among the Gentiles, write Scripture, and preach before governors and kings.

Whether people obtain a formal education or not, the Bible encourages the pursuit of spiritual training and scriptural study. In the Old Testament, prophets gathered in companies, assemblies, or schools to study the Word of God. Samuel headed one such school of the prophets (I Samuel 19:20). Elijah was closely associated with these students (II Kings 4:38-44; 6:1-7). King Jehoshaphat kindled revival throughout the country of Judah by sending princes, priests, and Levites into all the cities to teach God's Word to the people (II Chronicles 17:7-10).

In the New Testament, Jesus trained His twelve apostles intensively during His three-year ministry, using the Old Testament as His text. Paul studied under the great Jewish scholar Gamaliel and then spent three years of concentrated spiritual contemplation in Arabia (Acts 22:3; Galatians 1:17-18). He taught the Word of God for two years at a school in Ephesus (Acts 19:9-10).

To promote the apostolic message and ministry, the United Pentecostal Church International has endorsed eight Bible colleges in the U.S. and Canada, including one that operates in Spanish, and it has established one graduate school. The foundation of study for all these schools is the Bible, and each of them is committed to the apostolic doctrines of the new birth and holiness of life. At Urshan Graduate School of Theology, we emphasize a threefold purpose: to *prepare* men and women for Christian service, to *preserve* our apostolic doctrinal heritage, and to *propagate* the gospel of Jesus Christ worldwide. An apostolic education enables people to prepare more fully for service in God's kingdom and ultimately to fulfill the ministry that God has given them. Some will attend school full time, while others will take a few classes, perhaps through distance learning, as a supplement to what they are learning elsewhere.

In sum, education is one tool among many. The church can benefit from people with a diversity of educational backgrounds. God can use people in many ways whether or not they have pursued higher education. Those who have formal training must still hold firmly to Scripture as the final authority and rely supremely upon the power of the Holy Spirit to accomplish the work of God. Those who do not have formal training must still be diligent students of Scripture and of practical ministry in order to be effective. By working together, sharing our diverse talents and experiences, and seeking the move of God, we can face the challenges of the twenty-first century and experience great apostolic revival.

Pentecostal Herald, July 2006

CHAPTER 12

Communication in Marriage

Every marriage faces challenges, both externally and internally. Every couple has misunderstandings, differences of opinion, and disagreements. (If not, then only one of the two is thinking.) The key to meeting these challenges and handling these disagreements is communication.

With effective communication, every problem can be resolved, but without it, every problem is potentially a major one. In short, good communication is essential to a good marriage. Let's talk about some important aspects of effective communication.

Trust. We should assume the best about our spouse and refuse to jump to negative conclusions. We should trust our spouse to be loyal to us and speak with our best interests at heart, and we should act the same way toward her or him.

Honesty. A couple should resolve never to lie to one another. Honesty forms the basis of trust. Honesty does not mean being rude or saying everything we know or think, but it does mean being truthful when we speak.

Openness. A couple needs to create a climate that encourages the free expression of thoughts and feelings without violating a sense of security. They should be able to share their deepest desires, dreams, fears, and doubts, all within the context of unconditional love.

Respect and kindness. We should treat our spouse with courtesy, consideration, tact, and affection. We must always respect one another, and our words must communicate that respect. It is important for husband and wife to act worthy of respect as well as show respect, and to apologize if they ever violate this principle. Yelling, screaming, name calling, and harsh, offensive, or abusive speech or actions are never appropriate. Most people have learned to communicate with self-control and respect toward their boss, no matter how upset or offended they may be, because it is in their own interest to do so. How much more should we treat our marriage partner with respect and kindness, regardless of the circumstances!

Time and opportunity. Husband and wife need to spend time together. Quality time is important, but it cannot substitute for quantity. Many opportunities for good communication arise spontaneously when we spend much time together. It is also important to schedule quality time for communication without distraction. Plan a date once a week or twice a month!

Listening. Hearing each other is not enough; we must pay attention to each other. Good listening includes sensitivity and empathy. Instead of merely responding to the words that our spouse says, we should seek to understand the full message he or she is trying to communicate and the underlying needs being expressed.

70

For example, a woman may initiate a conversation with her husband about a discouraging event in her day. She wants sympathy, empathy, and a reaffirmation of her worth and value. Not realizing this, the husband may respond with a solution to the perceived problem or even a small lecture on how he would have handled things. The more she tries to explain how difficult the situation was, the more he offers advice. He is pleased with himself, because he is "communicating" with his wife and "helping" her. To his surprise, she reacts in frustration, because she is not asking him to be her teacher but her friend.

As this example illustrates, men need to discern when the conversation is more about expressing feelings than solving problems, and learn how to respond emotionally as well as rationally. Likewise, it is important to balance expressions of physical desire with expressions of romance. Similarly, the wife needs to learn what her husband is trying to express when he communicates.

When I married at age twenty-four, I had lived away from home for seven years, and for the last three of those I had lived alone in an efficiency apartment. My plans for dinner usually involved sitting at the table alone with a book or magazine. When we got married, my wife soon announced a new rule: No reading at the table. Dinner was a time to communicate.

Similarly, when I arrived home from work each day, my idea of relaxation was to sit in my easy chair with reading material for about an hour—or perhaps the whole evening. My wife wanted to share the events of the day, thoughts, and feelings. I would gladly oblige, letting her talk while I continued to read, and giving one-word replies when necessary. Occasionally, she would complain that I wasn't listening, but I usually managed to repeat a few of the words she had just said. I thought the situation was well under control.

One day, she had enough. She walked over to my chair where I was reading the newspaper and proceeded to sit in my lap—on top of the newspaper. Putting her face directly in front of mine, she said, "I'm your wife. Talk to me. And look at me when you talk to me."

That's how I learned to communicate with my wife. And I'm still learning.

Unpublished newsletter

CHAPTER 13

Should Christians Keep the Sabbath?

Groups such as the Seventh-day Adventists have raised many questions about the Sabbath in the minds of Christians. Should we still keep the seventh-day Sabbath of the Old Testament? Should we keep Sunday as the Sabbath? Has Sabbath keeping been abolished under the new covenant? What meaning does the Sabbath have for us today?

The Command and Its Significance

The command to keep the Sabbath was first given in the law of Moses and is part of the Ten Commandments (Exodus 20:8-11; Deuteronomy 5:12-15). The word *sabbath* comes from a Hebrew root that means "to rest, cease, desist, leave off" (Gesenius). On the pain of death, the Israelites were not to do any work on the Sabbath—not even cooking, lighting a fire, gathering firewood, or traveling. (See Exodus 16:23-30; 20:8-11; 31:12-17; 35:1-3; Numbers 15:32-36.) While the Sabbath was a day of worship, sacred assembly, and special sacrifices in the Tabernacle and Temple ("an holy convocation"), for the average person it was primarily a day of rest at home ("the sabbath of rest . . . in all your dwellings") (Leviticus 23:3). Historians agree that synagogues and local Sabbath worship at them did not come into existence until after the destruction of the Temple in 586 BC.

Several passages of Scripture disclose that the Sabbath was given uniquely to the nation of Israel: "Verily my sabbaths ye shall keep: for it is a sign between me and you throughout your generations; that ye may know that I am the LORD that doth sanctify you" (Exodus 31:13). (See Ezekiel 20:12-13.) "And remember that thou wast a servant in the land of Egypt, and that the LORD thy God brought thee out thence through a mighty hand and by a stretched out arm: therefore the LORD thy God commanded thee to keep the sabbath day" (Deuteronomy 5:15).

These passages also reveal a twofold significance for the Sabbath law. First, as we have already seen, the Sabbath provided a weekly day of rest from all work. It was instituted for people's physical, mental, and spiritual well-being, not because the day itself was sacred. As Jesus said, "The sabbath was made for man, and not man for the sabbath" (Mark 2:27). This provision of rest was especially significant to the Israelites, for the Sabbath was a constant, vivid reminder that God had delivered them from slavery and entered into covenant relationship with them.

Second, the Sabbath served to sanctify the nation of Israel, that is, to set it apart or separate it from all other nations, for no other nation observed the Sabbath. Along with laws concerning diet, farming practices, and clothing, the Sabbath law distinguished the Israelites from everyone else and identified them physically as Jehovah's chosen people.

The Sabbath and the New Covenant

The church today is not under God's covenant with Israel as epitomized by the Ten Commandments, but under the new covenant (Jeremiah 31:31-34; Romans 7:5-6; Galatians 3:23-25; 4:21-31). As a result, the church no longer observes the physical signs and ceremonies of the old covenant, such as circumcision (Galatians 6:15). God and His Word are unchanging, but some of His commands relate only to certain people or a certain time. While God's moral law never changes, Christians are not subject to the ceremonial law of the Old Testament. (See Mark 7:14-19; Acts 11:5-9; 15:1-29.)

The Jewish Sabbath was part of that ceremonial law; the Sabbath is not inherently moral. In Isaiah 1:10-20, God contrasted ceremonial observances—including blood sacrifices, feasts, and Sabbaths—with moral standards, saying He detested the Israelites' keeping of the former because they did not live up to the latter.

If Sabbath keeping were a universal, eternal, moral duty, God would not have expressed displeasure with it under any circumstances. Similarly, Jesus compared the Sabbath to other ceremonial law, which could be superseded even under the old covenant in cases of higher moral need (Matthew 12:1-13). Jesus and Paul affirmed the moral law of the Old Testament. They referred to some of the Ten Commandments as stating eternal moral standards, but it is notable that they did not mention the Sabbath law in these references (Mark 10:19; 12:28-31; Romans 13:8-10).

God used the ceremonial law—including blood sacrifices, dietary laws, circumcision, Sabbaths, and feasts—as types and shadows of truth to be found in Christ and His gospel. Since we now have the substance, or reality, we no longer need to observe the types and shadows. "Let no man therefore judge you in meat, or in drink, or in respect of an holyday, or of the new moon, or of the sabbath days: which are a shadow of things to come; but the body is of Christ" (Colossians 2:16-17).

Other New Testament passages also show that Sabbath keeping is not a requirement of the new covenant. It is permissible to regard a certain day as special, but it is wrong to make it a moral duty for oneself or others: "One man esteemeth one day above another: another esteemeth every day alike. Let every man be fully persuaded in his own mind. He that regardeth the day, regardeth it unto the Lord; and he that regardeth not the day, to the Lord he doth not regard it. . . . Let us not therefore judge one another any more" (Romans 14:5-6, 13). "How turn ye again to the weak and beggarly elements, whereunto ye desire again to be in bondage? Ye observe days, and months, and times, and years. I am afraid of you, lest I have bestowed upon you labour in vain" (Galatians 4:9-11).

Jesus observed the Sabbath because He was a Jew living under the old covenant. For the same reason, He was circumcised and observed the Jewish feast days. At the same time, Jesus claimed to be the Lord of the Sabbath, indicating that He could apply or change it as He saw fit (Mark 2:28).

At first, Jewish Christians apparently kept the Sabbath as part of their culture. In Acts 10-11, Peter and the Jewish church were still adhering to Jewish dietary laws for the same reason. In Acts 21, Paul underwent a Jewish purification ceremony, which included a Temple offering, in order to reassure Jews that he was not trying to destroy their culture. He also attended synagogues often in order to preach to Jews. But in Acts 15 the Jerusalem Council ruled that Gentile Christians did not have to keep the law of Moses, except for four items that they listed in a letter to all the Gentile churches. Significantly, the Sabbath was not one of them.

Some people point to the creation story as proof that the Sabbath law is eternal. God "ended his work" of creation and "rested" on the seventh day; moreover, He "blessed the seventh day, and sanctified it" (Genesis 2:2-3). When God gave the Ten Commandments, He cited this precedent as justification for the Sabbath law (Exodus 20:11; 31:17).

Since Genesis was one of the five books of the law originally written for Israel, the creation story was naturally used to support the Sabbath command to Israel. While the Genesis account indicates the need for a weekly day of rest, it does not command Sabbath observance as such. The Bible nowhere states that people before the law observed the Sabbath as a day of rest or worship. Moreover, due to many changes in calendars over the centuries it is impossible to say that the seventh day of Genesis 2 is the modern Saturday.

We should also note that the Bible nowhere indicates that the Sabbath has been changed to Sunday or that God intends for Sunday to be a new Christian Sabbath.

It should be pointed out that few persons keep the Sabbath law today. In order to do so, people could not perform any work or light a fire. Thus they could not use any type of stove, heater, internal combustion engine, or electricity. Moreover, they could not cause anyone else to violate the Sabbath, which they would do if they ate in a restaurant or used utilities, the telephone, or the radio.

Worship on Sunday

Christians are to be faithful to local church meetings whenever they are held (Hebrews 10:25), and any day is appropriate for a special spiritual observance (Romans 14:5-6).

From the earliest times, Christians have usually conducted their main worship services on Sunday. Early believers chose the day of Christ's resurrection to emphasize that they were not under the old covenant, which the Sabbath symbolized, but under the new covenant, which His resurrection instituted. Thus the believers at Troas met on the first day of the week for worship (Acts 20:7), and Paul instructed the Corinthians to collect offerings on the first day (I Corinthians 16:2). John was "in the Spirit on the Lord's day" when Jesus appeared to him in a vision (Revelation 1:10).

Jesus Himself established the precedent of meeting on the first day. Not only did He first appear to His assembled disciples on the evening of His resurrection day (John 20:19), but His next appearance to the group was on the same day one week later (John 20:26). ("After eight days" is reckoned in the ancient Jewish manner, counting both the starting and ending day.) And the Holy Spirit fell on the assembled disciples on Pentecost Sunday.

Sunday was a normal workday in the pagan Roman Empire, so Christians usually met in the early morning or in the evening. After Emperor Constantine made Christianity legal and then began supporting it, he proclaimed Sunday an official holiday. He did not originate Sunday worship but merely legalized and facilitated the existing practice. However, his action did encourage the view that Sunday was a new Christian Sabbath.

Spiritual Application

From the Sabbath law we can draw a principle of enduring importance and continuing application: the need to provide a time of rest for our bodies and our spirits. In addition, Colossians 2:16-17 speaks of a deeper significance, describing the Sabbath as a type or foreshadowing of a greater reality to be found in Christ. Like the Levitical sacrifices, the Sabbaths are fulfilled in Him.

In other words, the Sabbath points to the spiritual rest that Jesus promised: "Come unto me, all ye that labour and are heavy laden," He invited, "and I will give you rest. Take my yoke upon you, and learn of me; for I am meek and lowly in heart: and ye shall find rest unto your souls. For my yoke is easy, and my burden is light" (Matthew 11:28-30). Significantly, in the passage immediately after this statement, Jesus indicated that the Sabbath law was ceremonial in nature and asserted His lordship over it (Matthew 12:1-13).

It is specifically through the baptism of the Holy Spirit with the initial sign of speaking in tongues that we partake of the spiritual rest Christ provides. Isaiah 28:11-12 promises, "For with stammering lips and another tongue will he speak to this people. To whom he said, This is the rest wherewith ye may cause the weary to rest; and this is the refreshing."

The apostle Peter alluded to this promise when he preached in Acts 3:19, "Repent ye therefore, and be converted, that your sins may be blotted out, when the times

of refreshing shall come from the presence of the Lord."
The last clause of this verse describes the gift of the Holy
Spirit, as shown by Acts 2:38, a parallel statement from
another sermon of Peter's: "Repent, and be baptized
every one of you in the name of Jesus Christ for the
remission of sins, and ye shall receive the gift of the Holy
Ghost."

We also receive sanctification, or power to separate
from sin and identify with Christ, through the indwelling
Holy Spirit (II Thessalonians 2:13; I Peter 1:2). Just as
the physical Sabbath provided physical rest and sanctification for the Israelites under the old covenant, so the
indwelling Holy Spirit, the Spirit of Jesus Christ, provides
spiritual rest and sanctification for the church under the
new covenant. Just as the Sabbath was a constant
reminder of Israel's deliverance from bondage and of
their covenant relationship with God, so the Holy Spirit is
a constant reminder of our deliverance from sin and of
our new covenant relationship with God. The Spirit gives
us power over sin (Acts 1:8; Romans 8:4), and the Spirit
effects the new covenant in our hearts (II Corinthians
3:3; Hebrews 8:8-11). By living in the Spirit, we enjoy the
true Sabbath every day.

The enduring significance of the Sabbath is beauti-
fully described in Hebrews 3:7-4:11. Because of their
unbelief, the Israelites did not enter into the rest that God
provided for them, but the church today still has a
promise of spiritual rest. And according to Hebrews 4:4,
this spiritual rest is the true and ultimate fulfillment of
God's rest on the seventh day of creation.

Hebrews 4:9 states emphatically, "There remaineth
therefore a rest to the people of God." The word *rest* here

is a translation of the Greek word *sabbatismos*, which literally means a Sabbath keeping or a Sabbath rest (Thayer). Does this verse refer to physical Old Testament Sabbath observance? No. The next verse states that our Sabbath consists of resting, or ceasing, from our works, just as God did from His (Hebrew 4:10). In other words, to enjoy true spiritual rest, we must renounce the works of the flesh and stop trying to earn salvation by our own works. Instead, we must exercise faith in Christ's work on our behalf. Through faith, we receive His Holy Spirit and live daily by the Spirit's guidance and power. The Spirit works in us to regenerate and sanctify, thus preparing us for the eternal Sabbath rest.

Of course, true faith is not passive; it is an active reliance upon God that issues forth in obedience. Thus Hebrews 4:11 admonishes, "Let us labour [be diligent, make every effort] therefore to enter into that rest, lest any man fall after the same example of unbelief."

Yes, we have a Sabbath rest—the refreshing presence and sanctifying power of the Holy Spirit that we enjoy every day. And, yes, the ultimate Sabbath rest awaits us still—eternal rest in the presence of the One to whom the Old Testament Sabbath points: Jesus Christ our Lord.

Pentecostal Herald, December 1988 and March 2001; Word Aflame Press tract, 1989

CHAPTER 14

Moral Values in Society
Why We Should Not Support Homosexual Marriage

God created one man and one woman to inhabit the Garden of Eden, and He created them as companions who were suitable for each other. We must uphold that ideal for marriage today, but how should we do so in modern society?

Let us briefly consider the biblical teaching on this subject. The Genesis account, as reiterated by Jesus, establishes that God's plan for marriage is for a man and a woman to form a new, exclusive, permanent, and public partnership for life in which they are joined together physically, emotionally, and spiritually. (See Genesis 2:18-25; Matthew 19:3-6.) God has made it abundantly clear that homosexual activity is sinful and cannot fulfill His intention for marriage. (See Genesis 19:1-11; Leviticus 18:22; 20:13; I Kings 15:11-12; Romans 1:26-27; I Corinthians 6:9-10; I Timothy 1:10; Jude 7.)

Of course, not everyone accepts biblical morality. We live in a pluralistic society—one in which people have many different religious and moral beliefs. In such a society, the government cannot and should not try to impose morality in people's private lives.

Nevertheless, it is simply wrong to say that we cannot base our laws upon moral values. We do it all the time. Specifically, when moral wrongs hurt other people, or when moral issues negatively affect society as a whole, we have a right and responsibility to implement moral values.

For instance, most people agree that stealing and killing are wrong. This is a moral position, not a scientific one. For example, the theory of evolution cannot teach us that these practices are wrong. If given the opportunity, one animal will steal food from another animal, kill another animal, and even eat another animal. No one considers these actions to be morally wrong; it is simply the nature of animals to do these things. Moreover, some people believe that stealing and killing are acceptable under certain circumstances. For instance, the followers of Osama bin Laden kill "infidels," and Marxists such as Lenin, Stalin, and Mao made stealing and killing part of their social order. Regardless of people's private beliefs, however, the law of the land prohibits these actions, and it does so because of a Judeo-Christian (that is, a biblical) understanding of right and wrong.

As another example, most people seem to think that lying is acceptable under certain circumstances or at least a minor wrong that should not be punished. Nevertheless, when lying hurts other people economically or undermines the social order, we have laws against it. If individuals cheat on their income tax, or if executives lie about the assets of their company, they can go to jail. In short, our society recognizes that the government has the right and responsibility to pass and enforce laws based on moral values.

Some say that sexual morality is completely different, claiming that personal choices in this area do not affect the rest of society. Our pluralistic society has decided not to regulate what two consenting adults do in the privacy of a home, because their action does not seem to affect anyone else directly. Therefore, we no longer have laws against fornication, adultery, or homosexual behavior (even though these actions can drastically affect a family).

Now, however, some homosexuals are asking for a legal right to marry. It is important to recognize that such a change in our laws *would* affect society significantly.

Recognizing homosexual marriage would mean social endorsement of homosexuality, and that is really what homosexual activists want. They already have the freedom for consenting relationships, but they want the rest of society to state that these relationships are acceptable, that is, morally good. In effect, they are trying to legislate their own version of morality and impose it on the majority who disagree.

They incorrectly claim that opponents are homophobic and that homosexual marriage is a matter of civil rights. This is the language of morality. The choice is not whether to legislate morality or not, because either way a certain version of morality will be enshrined in the law. The real issue is which moral view will prevail. What moral statement will we make as a nation and as a society?

This issue becomes clear when we look at the ultimate source of human rights. The U.S. Declaration of Independence states, "We hold these Truths to be self-evident, that all Men are created equal, that they are endowed by their Creator with certain unalienable

Rights." In the final analysis, any appeal for civil rights is an appeal to an understanding of morality and theology.

The issue of whose morality will become the law of the land is not abstract. Creating something known as homosexual marriage would affect everyone in several significant ways.

First, it would mean social endorsement of homosexuality and in effect would promote this lifestyle. It would send a powerful and negative message to children, youth, people struggling with their identity, and people striving to fulfill God's plan.

When a sin is generally recognized as sin, some still practice it, but many receive strength to rise above temptation. In our day, many children have been raised in dysfunctional families, and many teenagers have had unfortunate experiences of abuse or manipulation. In a society that actively promotes homosexuality, some of them will experiment with behavior that otherwise they would not have chosen, and some will proceed into a lifestyle that otherwise would not have been an option. The resulting spiritual devastation will be incalculable.

Second, it would create significant legal and financial benefits for homosexual couples, to the detriment of society as a whole. Our legal structure recognizes the uniqueness of marriage in a host of areas, including income taxes, insurance, retirement, death benefits, medical decisions, inheritance, child custody, and other spousal and parental rights. If we recognize homosexual marriage, then we will make a decision to apply these special provisions to homosexual relationships and to spend money to support them. Government agencies, charitable organizations, and private businesses will be forced to extend all marital provisions to homosexual couples.

For millennia, humans have recognized that heterosexual unions are the basis for families and that families are the building blocks of society. This truth is rooted in two biological and social realities. First, it takes a man and a woman to bring children in existence. Second, men and women are physically and mentally different and thus make unique contributions to the nurturing and training of children. They are complementary partners in building marriages, homes, families, and society in a way that two men or two women cannot be.

Consequently, human society has always deemed that the family is uniquely deserving of support in many ways. Strong families based upon the committed marriage of a husband and a wife provide the best means of raising children who are physically, mentally, and spiritually healthy and who become stable, productive citizens. While we offer support to people who find themselves in less than ideal circumstances through death or divorce, we recognize that it is in the best interests of society as a whole to promote strong families based on the union of a man and a woman.

As a practical example, if homosexual marriage becomes legal, then homosexual activists will demand that public schools endorse their moral views in classes, counseling, and public activities. They will insist that the public school system uphold the law by teaching children that homosexual marriage is morally correct.

Already, some high school counselors advocate homosexuality as an option for confused teens and promote acceptance of homosexuality generally. Recently, a high school student in Austin, Texas, was required to review stories of romance for an English class, and he was specifically instructed to include homosexual romance and treat it favorably in his report. If homosexual marriage were to become legal, students and parents would no longer have the right to protest such practices. Christians would no longer have the right to present another view.

Third, biblical marriage would be devalued. More and more, people would cease to regard heterosexual marriage as uniquely deserving of full moral, social, legal, and economic support. We are already seeing this effect in Scandinavia and the Netherlands, which offer legal unions for homosexuals. In these countries, there has been a significant decline in marriage and a significant increase in children being born and raised out of wedlock.

Fourth, homosexual marriage would set a legal precedent for further changes in the definition of marriage. It would assist people who want public, legal endorsement of other moral choices such as polygamy, incest, bestiality, and sex with minors (statutory rape). Groups have already formed to promote such practices, one example being the North American Man-Boy Love Association. Such groups could employ the same legal arguments as homosexuals, asserting rights to privacy, personal choice, and social approval for all sexual practices.

Fifth, we could expect attempts to curtail freedom of speech, press, assembly, and religion. The reason is that the conflict is not over private practices but over public endorsement. Therefore, homosexual activists will not be content until they are successful in suppressing opposing views. They will use social ridicule, ostracism, and, if possible, legal persecution to marginalize and silence Christians.

This process has already begun. For example, in Sweden a minister was arrested for preaching against homosexuality. In Canada, someone was fined for placing Scripture references against homosexuality in a newspaper advertisement. There have already been threats that if ministers refuse to endorse homosexual marriage, the government could take away their right to perform legal marriages. In Pennsylvania, people who protested publicly against homosexuality were arrested for hate speech. Fortunately, a judge released them in recognition that the First Amendment of the U.S. Constitution protects freedom of speech in precisely these circumstances. However, it is possible that activist judges could reinterpret the provisions of the First Amendment contrary to the intention of the framers, just as they are attempting to redefine the concept of marriage itself contrary to biblical, social, and legal precedent.

As Christians, we must treat all people with dignity and respect, and we should acknowledge that many homosexuals are productive citizens, albeit deceived by sin. At the same time, we must stand for truth. We need to offer the hope of a new life with power to overcome sin and its destructive consequences. We must take a clear stand against fornication, adultery, and homosexuality and a clear stand for biblical marriage. We need to exert a positive moral influence upon our society and make our voice heard with regard to political decisions that affect the moral values of society. Individuals have the right to choose their own lifestyle, but collectively we have the right to choose what moral views our society should endorse. Most of all, we should seek to win the hearts of people one at a time as they respond to the gospel and are changed by the power of God. As the church, we are called to be the salt of the earth and the light of the world.

Pentecostal Herald, August 2005

CHAPTER 15

The Blessed Hope

Looking for the blessed hope and glorious appearing of our great God and Savior Jesus Christ (Titus 2:13, NKJV).

The hope of the church is the coming of the Lord Jesus Christ for His saints. That is the next great event in God's plan for humanity.

The first-century church expected the Lord to come back in their day. The apostle Paul wrote, "For this we say to you by the word of the Lord, that we who are alive and remain until the coming of the Lord will by no means precede those who are asleep. For the Lord Himself will descend from heaven with a shout, with the voice of an archangel, and with the trumpet of God. And the dead in Christ will rise first. Then we who are alive and remain shall be caught up together with them in the clouds to meet the Lord in the air. And thus we shall always be with the Lord" (I Thessalonians 4:15-17, NKJV).

Paul spoke as if he would be alive when the Lord came to catch away His saints. He lived with expectancy that the Lord could return in his day.

The modern Pentecostal movement began as people began to seek the baptism of the Holy Spirit in anticipation of the soon return of Jesus Christ. They read the preaching of the apostle Peter in Acts 2 that in the last days God would pour out His Spirit on all flesh. They read the prophecy that Peter quoted from Joel 2, in which God promised a former rain and a latter rain. They concluded that the former rain was the Day of Pentecost and the latter rain would be the final outpouring of the Spirit before the coming of the Lord. As a result, they experienced a mighty Holy Ghost revival. Indeed, historians say that the two most significant beliefs of the early Pentecostal movement were the baptism of the Holy Spirit and the second coming of Jesus Christ.

The Lord did not come back in Paul's day, nor did He come back in the early twentieth century. Were the believers of these two centuries wrong to look for His coming? Not at all! It is God's will for every generation of believers to anticipate His soon return.

When we lose that expectancy, we become self-centered and apathetic about the things of God. But when we keep our focus on the Lord's return, we maintain a sense of divine destiny and live by heavenly priorities. We realize that we are indeed strangers and pilgrims in this world (Hebrews 11:13). Therefore, instead of seeking ultimate satisfaction in things that are temporary, we place our hope in the world to come. Instead of living primarily to please people today and to succeed in secular affairs, we strive to prepare for our eternal destiny.

We cannot know exactly when the Lord will return (Matthew 24:36). With the Lord, a day is as a thousand years, and a thousand years as a day (II Peter 3:8). There-fore, what seems like a long delay to us is just a short passage of time to Him. When He is ready, His coming will be swift, and it will come upon this world unexpectedly as a thief in the night. Although we do not know when Jesus will return, He identified various signs that would characterize the time of His coming. (See Matthew 24:4-8.) The increasing intensity of these signs in our day convinces us that the coming of the Lord is indeed drawing near.

The soon coming of the Lord motivates us to reach out a lost world. In the last chapter of the Bible, Jesus announced, "Behold, I come quickly; and my reward is with me, to give every man according as his work shall be" (Revelation 22:12). The response to this announcement is a call to salvation: "The Spirit and the bride say, Come. And let him that heareth say, Come. And let him that is athirst come. And whosoever will, let him take the water of life freely" (Revelation 22:17).

The soon coming of the Lord also motivates us to live a holy life. When we realize that this world and everything in it will soon pass away, we understand the importance of holy conduct and godliness (II Peter 3:11). "Therefore, beloved, looking forward to these things, be diligent to be found by Him in peace, without spot and blameless" (II Peter 3:14, NKJV).

Let's get ready for the coming of our great God and Savior Jesus Christ. This is our blessed hope!

South Texas Vision, May-June 2005

DOCTRINE

CHAPTER 16

The Apostles' Doctrine

And they continued stedfastly in the apostles' doctrine (Acts 2:42).

If we will continue steadfastly in apostolic identity and unity, which are based upon doctrinal truth, we will have apostolic revival.

The Importance of Doctrine

Doctrine simply means the teaching of God's Word. In our day most people do not want to hear sound doctrine, but they only want preachers who will make them feel good (II Timothy 4:3). Nevertheless, we must love, cherish, and obey the Word of God. Merely knowing and mentally accepting the truth is not enough; in order to escape delusion and condemnation we must have a love for the truth (II Thessalonians 2:10-12). Therefore, Paul admonished ministers, "Preach the word; be instant in season, out of season; reprove, rebuke, exhort with all longsuffering and doctrine" (II Timothy 4:2).

By becoming established in doctrinal truth, we fulfill the scriptural admonitions (1) to be studious (diligent) workers approved of God, who are not ashamed but who rightly divide (correctly handle) the Word of truth (II Timothy 2:15); (2) to use Scripture profitably for doctrine, reproof, correction, and instruction in righteousness (II Timothy 3:16); (3) to be strong in our beliefs rather than tossed about by every wind of doctrine (Ephesians 4:14); and (4) to give answers to everyone who asks about our faith (I Peter 3:15).

Some erroneously suppose that doctrinal study deadens spirituality, but a sincere, prayerful study of biblical doctrine will enhance spirituality. In fact, true spirituality can only develop from a solid understanding of God's Word. The truth sets us free spiritually (John 8:32). The more we comprehend divine principles, the more God's power will operate in our lives and in our churches.

Another erroneous assumption is that there is little connection between doctrinal beliefs and conduct. To the contrary, what we believe will definitely determine our conduct. Inadequate or false doctrinal views affect the actions we take and the choices we make. The more we assimilate divine principles, the more Christ-like we will become in daily life.

The way to grow to maturity in the faith is to have a balance of doctrine and spirituality. We must be as zealous to hear, read, and study God's Word as we are to worship God and have fellowship with each other. We must be as zealous to pray and worship as we are to study and receive teaching.

The Apostolic Message

What important doctrines did the apostles proclaim? What should we believe, obey, and love? For an initial answer to these questions, let us look briefly at the apostle Peter's preaching on the Day of Pentecost. This message is important for several reasons: it was the first sermon of the New Testament church (i.e., after the outpouring of the Spirit), Jesus had ordained Peter to open the doors of the kingdom of heaven with this message, it had the simultaneous support of all twelve apostles, and it proclaims in a nutshell how to enter the New Testament church.

The doctrine of God: There is one true God, as proclaimed in the Old Testament, and in the last days He wants to pour out His Spirit upon everyone. (See Acts 2:17; Deuteronomy 6:4.)

The doctrine of Jesus Christ: Jesus died, was buried, and rose again for our salvation. He is both Lord and Messiah—both the one true God and the sinless, perfect, anointed Man through whom God reveals Himself to us. In other words, Jesus is God manifested in flesh to be our Savior. (See Acts 2:21-36; Colossians 2:9-10.)

The doctrine of salvation: We enter into the New Testament church through faith in Jesus as Lord and Savior, repentance from sin, water baptism in the name of Jesus Christ, and the baptism of the Holy Spirit with the initial sign of tongues. (See Acts 2:1-4, 36-39; 11:13-17.)

The doctrine of holiness and Christian living: We must separate ourselves from sin and worldly values and dedicate ourselves to God and His will. The new life of holiness will transform us both inwardly and outwardly. It is characterized by prayer, fellowship, giving, joyful worship, miraculous gifts of the Spirit, and evangelism. (See Acts 2:40, 42-47; Hebrews 12:14.)

The doctrine of eternal judgment: The Lord is coming back for His people, with eternal punishment for the unrighteous and eternal reward for the righteous. (See Acts 2:19-21; Revelation 22:12-21.)

If we will proclaim, believe, and obey the apostles' doctrine, we will be saved, and our churches will have revival until Jesus comes!

South Texas Vision, March-April 2005

CHAPTER 17

Oneness Perspectives on the Incarnation

The Basic Oneness Position

Oneness believers hold that God is absolutely and indivisibly one.[1] Thus, they do not accept the idea of three distinct centers of consciousness in the Godhead. They also affirm that in Jesus dwells all the fullness of the Godhead bodily and that Jesus is the only name given for salvation.[2] The Father was revealed to the world in the name of Jesus, the Son was given the name of Jesus at birth, and the Holy Spirit comes to believers in the name of Jesus.[3] Thus the apostles correctly fulfilled Christ's command to baptize "in the name [singular] of the Father, and of the Son, and of the Holy Ghost" by baptizing all converts with the invocation of the name of Jesus.[4]

Oneness believers affirm that God has revealed Himself as Father (in parental relationship to humanity), in the Son (in human flesh), and as the Holy Spirit (in spiritual action).[5] They acknowledge that the one God existed as Father, Word, and Holy Spirit before His incarnation as Jesus Christ, the Son of God; and that while Jesus walked on earth as God Himself incarnate, the Spirit of God continued to be omnipresent.

Oneness Christology

Like trinitarians, Oneness believers confess that Jesus is true God and true man. The Incarnation joined the fullness of deity to complete humanity, resulting in one divine-human person. We can distinguish these two aspects of Christ's identity, but we cannot separate them.

The Oneness view differs from trinitarianism, however, in stressing that Jesus is the incarnation of the full, undivided Godhead,[6] not merely the incarnation of one of three divine persons. When the Old Testament speaks of the Messiah as "God," it does so in the context of absolute monotheism. Likewise, when the New Testament speaks of Jesus as "God," it does so with the Old Testament definition of "God." As to His eternal deity, there can be no subordination of Jesus to anyone else, whether in essence or position.

By contrast, trinitarian scholar Norman Geisler stated that, for technical accuracy, trinitarians should not say that "God" was manifested in the flesh but that "God the Son" was manifested in the flesh.[7] Citing I Timothy 3:16, Oneness believers emphatically proclaim that the former phrase, not the latter, is accurate.[8]

Turning to the humanity of Christ, Oneness believers agree with trinitarians that Jesus possessed all the elements of authentic humanity as originally created by God. Thus we can speak of Jesus as human in body, soul, spirit, mind, will, and so on.[9] According to the flesh, Jesus was the biological descendant of Adam and Eve, Abraham, David, and Mary.[10] We must not speak of two spirits in Jesus, however, but of one Spirit in which deity and humanity are joined.

Christ's humanity means that everything we humans can say of ourselves, we can say of Jesus in His earthly life, except for sin. Moreover, in every way that we relate to God, Jesus related to God, except that He did not need to repent or be born again. Thus, when Jesus prayed, when He submitted His will to the Father, and when He spoke of "my God, and your God" (John 20:17), He simply acted in accordance with His genuine humanity.

Trinitarians, however, see these examples as proving that the Father and the Son are two distinct persons. This difference of interpretation lies at the heart of the Oneness-trinitarian controversy. Most of the passages that trinitarians cite to demonstrate a distinction of persons, Oneness believers interpret as relating to the human identity of Jesus Christ.

The Trinity in Light of the Incarnation

We can go so far as to say that the trinitarian doctrine stands or falls on the New Testament distinction between the Father and the Son. The Old Testament does not explicitly teach the doctrine of the trinity. The New Testament says very little that could distinguish the Father and the Holy Spirit as two persons. The strongest texts that could establish a trinity are those in the New Testament, particularly in the Gospels, that make some sort of distinction between the Father and the Son. If the focus of these passages is the genuine humanity of Christ and not trinitarian distinctions, then the doctrine of the trinity loses it strongest support.

At this point, we need to define the trinitarian distinction of persons. According to classical trinitarian thought as formulated by the Cappadocian theologians of the fourth century, the one Godhead mysteriously subsists in three coequal, coeternal, coessential persons. There is communion of substance but distinction of personhood. This trinity is a perfect, inseparable union, and the persons work together in all things. The unique distinguishing characteristics of the persons are as follows: the Father is unbegotten, the Son is begotten, and the Holy Spirit is proceeding. The generation of the Son and the procession of the Holy Spirit are mysteries, however. While the persons are coequal and coeternal, the Father is in some sense the head and the origin.[11]

As trinitarian scholars have pointed out, much of this formulation has no objective, understandable meaning to us. Church historian Jaroslav Pelikan commented on the problem:

> This puzzling, indeed frustrating, combination of philosophical terminology for the relation of One and Three . . . was simultaneously typical of the theology of the Cappadocians and normative for the subsequent history of Trinitarian doctrine. . . . [The] answer to . . . difficult[ies] was to declare that what was common to the Three and what was distinctive among them lay beyond speech and comprehension and therefore beyond either analysis or conceptualization.[12]

Trinitarian scholar Harold O. J. Brown likewise acknowledged "that the properties *explain nothing*; on the contrary, they are merely conceptual tools or symbols to impress on us that the three Persons are and remain eternally distinct, yet also remain eternally one God."[13]

Despite its difficulties, this view is the position of trinitarianism today.[14] In a textbook published by the Assemblies of God, Kerry McRoberts identified these unique personal properties as necessary to distinguish trinitarianism from modalism, even though he acknowledged that they do not offer an explanation of the trinity.[15]

Although trinitarians say that the unique property of each divine person is a mystery, perhaps we can explore the claimed distinctions by posing a hypothetical question, within the trinitarian framework: In principle, based on what we know about the nature of God, could the Father have become incarnate? Or is incarnation a unique action that only the Son could have taken? Let us examine the two alternatives.

1. If we say that the Father could *not* have become incarnate, then we have apparently discovered a further distinction between the persons, one that classical trinitarianism does not proclaim. Unfortunately, it would make the divine persons different in essence, contrary to orthodox trinitarian doctrine.

Specifically, the Son would be inferior to the Father. Indeed, some ancient writers held, in accordance with Greek philosophy, that the supreme God, being perfect and holy, could not have direct contact with the world of matter. They identified the Father as the supreme God and the Son as a lesser deity. As Origen (c. AD 220) explained in refuting Oneness concepts of his time, "Some individuals among the multitude of believers . . .

incautiously assert that the Saviour is the Most High God; however, we do not hold with them; but rather believe Him when He says, 'The Father who sent Me is greater than I.'"[16]

Justin Martyr (c. AD 150) did not believe that the Father could manifest Himself even as a theophany, because it would not be suitable for Him to descend to our level. Only the Son could do so.[17] Eusebius of Caesarea (c. AD 330) similarly argued that the Father is too pure to unite Himself to corruptible flesh except by an intermediary power, namely, the Word.[18]

Finally, this line of reasoning concedes that the uniqueness of the Son lies in the Incarnation, rather than in the eternal generation that trinitarianism teaches. If we reject the subordinationism of the foregoing writers, then we are led to the Oneness position, for it defines the Son in terms of the Incarnation while rejecting any subordination of Jesus as to His divine nature.

2. On the other hand, could the Father *have* become incarnate? Most trinitarian scholars today would probably say yes. One of the foremost Roman Catholic theologians of the twentieth century, Karl Rahner, stated, "Since the time of Augustine, the theology of the schools has become accustomed to thinking that it is to be taken for granted that any one of the non-numerical three whom we call the persons of the one God-head could become man."[19]

If the Father had become incarnate, what would have been the nature of that incarnation? Would heaven have been devoid of the Father during His earthly manifestation? Surely not. The Father would have related in some fashion to the humanity that He thereby assumed. Would this human person have been born of a virgin? It seems that the nature of incarnation would have required it. Who would have been the Father of this child? Surely the Father. Would this man have prayed to the Father? Would he have obeyed the will of the Father? It seems that he would have done these things in order to be a righteous and holy man.

In other words, this divine-human person would necessarily have related to the Father in the same way that Jesus related to the Father as recorded in the Gospels. In short, the biblical distinction between the Son and the Father has nothing to do with persons in the Godhead, but it has everything to do with the Incarnation. The begetting of the Son occurred at the Incarnation; it is not an eternal, incomprehensible process within the Godhead. Thus there is no reason to explain the Gospel accounts of the Father and the Son in terms of a trinity.

The conclusion is that the Father *did* become incarnate—in Christ. According to I John 3:1-5, the Father manifested Himself to take away our sins, and He will appear to us again one day.

Notes

[1]Deuteronomy 6:4; Galatians 3:20.

[2]Colossians 2:9; Acts 4:12.

[3]Matthew 1:21; John 5:43; 14:26; 17:6.

[4]Matthew 28:19; Acts 2:38; 8:16; 10:48; 19:5; 22:16.

[5]See, for example, Deuteronomy 32:6 and Isaiah 63:16 (Father); Luke 1:35 and Galatians 4:4 (Son); Genesis 1:2 and Acts 1:8 (Holy Spirit).

[6]Colossians 2:9. Significantly, this passage uses three words that are logically redundant to emphasize this position: "all," "fullness," and "Godhead."

[7]Norman Geisler, lecture at the Symposium on Cults, the Occult,

and World Religions (sponsored by Apologetic Research Coalition, William Tyndale College, Farmington Hills, Mich., November 1988).

[8]Even if we adopt the alternate reading of "He was manifest in the flesh," we still must ask what is the antecedent of the pronoun "he." It appears in the preceding verse: "God." The alternative proposed by trinitarians—"Son of God"—does not appear in the entire book.

[9]See Matthew 26:38; Luke 2:40; 22:42; 23:46; John 1:14; Acts 2:31; Philippians 2:5; Hebrews 10:5, 10.

[10]See Genesis 3:15; Galatians 3:16; 4:4; Romans 1:3; Hebrews 2:14-17; 5:7-8.

[11]See Basil, *On the Spirit* 16:37-38 and *Letters*, 38, in Philip Schaff and Henry Wace, eds., *The Nicene and Post-Nicene Fathers*, 2d series [hereinafter *NPNF*] (Reprint, Grand Rapids: Eerdmans, 1976), 8:23-24, 137-40; Gregory of Nyssa, *On the Holy Spirit* and *On the Holy Trinity*, *NPNF* 5:314-30; Gregory of Nazianzus, *Third Theological Oration, On the Son* 29:3 and *Fifth Theological Oration, On the Holy Spirit*, 8-10, *NPNF* 7:301-2, 320-21.

[12]Jaroslav Pelikan, *The Christian Tradition: A History of the Development of Doctrine* (Chicago: University of Chicago Press, 1971), 1:223.

[13]Harold O. J. Brown, *Heresies: The Image of Christ in the Mirror of Heresy and Orthodoxy from the Apostles to the Present* (Garden City, N.J.: Doubleday, 1984), 151, emphasis in original.

[14]Louis Berkhof, *Systematic Theology*, 4th ed. (Grand Rapids: Eerdmans, 1941), 89.

[15]Kerry D. McRoberts, "The Holy Trinity," in Stanley Horton, ed., *Systematic Theology* (Springfield, Mo.: Gospel Publishing House, 1994), 167.

[16]Origen, *Against Celsus* 8:14, in Alexander Roberts, James Donaldson, and A. Cleveland Coxe, eds., *The Ante-Nicene Fathers* [hereinafter *ANF*] (1885; repr. Grand Rapids: Eerdmans, 1981), 4:644.

[17]Justin, *Dialogue with Trypho* 127:13, in *ANF* 1:263.

[18]Eusebius of Caesarea, *Oration in Praise of Constantine* 11:11:5-7, in *NPNF* 1:596-97.

[19]Karl Rahner, *Foundations of Christian Faith: An Introduction to the Idea of Christianity*, trans. William Dych (New York: Seabury Press, 1978), 214.

Forward, Fall 1999. Excerpted from a paper presented at the annual meeting of the Society for Pentecostal Studies, Evangel University, Springfield, Mo., March 11-13, 1999.

CHAPTER 18

The True Humanity of Jesus Christ

Teaching of Scripture

1. *Jesus was a true human being in every way, yet without sin. As such, He was born with the same kind of human identity that Adam and Eve had when they were first created.* "So God created man in his own image, in the image of God created he him; male and female created he them. . . . And God saw every thing that he had made, and, behold, it was very good" (Genesis 1:27, 31). "And the Word was made flesh, and dwelt among us, (and we beheld his glory, the glory as of the only begotten of the Father,) full of grace and truth" (John 1:14). "And ye know that he was manifested to take away our sins; and in him is no sin. . . . Hereby know ye the Spirit of God: Every spirit that confesseth that Jesus Christ is come in the flesh is of God" (I John 3:5; 4:2). "And without controversy great is the mystery of godliness: God was manifest in the flesh" (I Timothy 3:16). In the Bible, "flesh" usually refers to complete humanity, not merely a body. Jesus did not come in a different kind of flesh from ours, but in the same kind of flesh that we

have. "For he taught his disciples, and said unto them, The Son of man is delivered into the hands of men, and they shall kill him; and after that he is killed, he shall rise the third day" (Mark 9:31). In the phrase "Son of man," the Greek word for "man" is *anthropos*, which means "human being." Thus, Jesus is the Son of humanity as well as the Son of God. He is part of the human race, the race that descends from Adam and Eve.

2. *It was necessary for Jesus to come as one of us, with our kind of flesh and blood, and yet without sin, in order to be our high priest and to reconcile us to God.* "Forasmuch then as the children are partakers of flesh and blood, he also himself likewise took part of the same; that through death he might destroy him that had the power of death, that is, the devil; and deliver them who through fear of death were all their lifetime subject to bondage. For verily he took not on him the nature of angels; but he took on him the seed of Abraham. Wherefore in all things it behoved him to be made like unto his brethren, that he might be a merciful and faithful high priest in things pertaining to God, to make reconciliation for the sins of the people. For in that he himself hath suffered being tempted, he is able to succour them that are tempted" (Hebrews 2:14-18). "Seeing then that we have a great high priest, that is passed into the heavens, Jesus the Son of God, let us hold fast our profession. For we have not an high priest which cannot be touched with the feeling of our infirmities; but was in all points tempted like as we are, yet without sin" (Hebrews 4:14-15).

3. *Biologically, Jesus did not inherit sin, because at His conception the Holy Spirit performed a miracle to ensure that He would be holy. Legally, Jesus did not*

inherit sin, because sin is reckoned from the father, and the Father of Jesus was God. "And the angel answered and said unto her, The Holy Ghost shall come upon thee, and the power of the Highest shall over-shadow thee: therefore also that holy thing which shall be born of thee shall be called the Son of God" (Luke 1:35). In our case, sin is reckoned from Adam as the father, not Eve, even though Eve sinned first. "Wherefore, as by one man sin entered into the world, and death by sin; and so death passed upon all men, for that all have sinned: (For until the law sin was in the world: but sin is not imputed when there is no law. Nevertheless death reigned from Adam to Moses, even over them that had not sinned after the similitude of Adam's transgression, who is the figure of him that was to come)" (Romans 5:12-14).

4. *Jesus was the biological descendant of Adam and Eve.* "And I will put enmity between thee [the ser-pent] and the woman, and between thy seed and her seed; it shall bruise thy head, and thou shalt bruise his heel" (Genesis 3:15).

5. *Jesus was the biological descendant of Abra-ham.* "Now to Abraham and his seed were the promises made. He saith not, And to seeds, as of many; but as of one, And to thy seed, which is Christ" (Galatians 3:16). "For verily he took not on him the nature of angels; but he took on him the seed of Abraham" (Hebrews 2:16). The Greek word for "seed" in these passages is *sperma*, from which we get the English word *sperm*.

6. *Jesus was a natural Israelite in the same way as Paul.* "For I could wish that myself were accursed from Christ for my brethren, my kinsmen according to the flesh: who are Israelites; to whom pertaineth the

adoption, and the glory, and the covenants, and the giving of the law, and the service of God, and the promises; whose are the fathers, and of whom as concerning the flesh Christ came, who is over all, God blessed for ever. Amen" (Romans 9:3-5).

7. *Jesus was the biological descendant of David.* "Men and brethren, let me freely speak unto you of the patriarch David, that he is both dead and buried, and his sepulchre is with us unto this day. Therefore being a prophet, and knowing that God had sworn with an oath to him, that of the fruit of his loins, according to the flesh, he would raise up Christ to sit on his throne; he seeing this before spake of the resurrection of Christ, that his soul was not left in hell, neither his flesh did see corruption. This Jesus hath God raised up, whereof we all are witnesses" (Acts 2:29-32). "Concerning his Son Jesus Christ our Lord, which was made of the seed of David according to the flesh" (Romans 1:3). "Hath not the scripture said, That Christ cometh of the seed of David, and out of the town of Bethlehem, where David was?" (John 7:42). "I Jesus have sent mine angel to testify unto you these things in the churches. I am the root and the offspring of David, and the bright and morning star" (Revelation 22:16).

8. *Jesus is the biological descendant of Mary, who, as the angels confessed, was His true mother.* "And, behold, thou shalt conceive in thy womb, and bring forth a son, and shalt call his name JESUS" (Luke 1:31). "But when the fulness of the time was come, God sent forth his Son, made of a woman, made under the law" (Galatians 4:4). "And when they were come into the house, they saw the young child with Mary his mother, and fell

down, and worshipped him. . . . And when they were departed, behold, the angel of the Lord appeareth to Joseph in a dream, saying, Arise, and take the young child and his mother, and flee into Egypt, and be thou there until I bring thee word: for Herod will seek the young child to destroy him. . . . But when Herod was dead, behold, an angel of the Lord appeareth in a dream to Joseph in Egypt, saying, Arise, and take the young child and his mother, and go into the land of Israel: for they are dead which sought the young child's life" (Matthew 2:11, 13, 19-20). Since Jesus was born of Mary, He had the same kind of humanity that we have, for "that which is born of the flesh is flesh" (John 3:6).

9. *As a human, Jesus grew mentally, physically, spiritually, and socially.* "And Jesus increased in wisdom and stature, and in favor with God and men" (Luke 2:52, NKJV).

10. *Jesus was human in will.* There was a distinction between the human will of Christ and the divine will. "And he went a little further, and fell on his face, and prayed, saying, O my Father, if it be possible, let this cup pass from me: nevertheless not as I will, but as thou wilt" (Matthew 26:39).

11. *Jesus was human in soul.* "He hath poured out his soul unto death: and he was numbered with the transgressors; and he bare the sin of many, and made intercession for the transgressors" (Isaiah 53:12). "Then saith he unto them, My soul is exceeding sorrowful, even unto death: tarry ye here, and watch with me" (Matthew 26:38).

12. *Jesus was human in spirit.* There was a distinction between the human spirit of Christ and the divine

Spirit (the Father), although not a separation, so that we can say humanity and deity were joined in the one Spirit of Christ. "And when Jesus had cried with a loud voice, he said, Father, into thy hands I commend my spirit: and having said thus, he gave up the ghost" (Luke 23:46). "How much more shall the blood of Christ, who through the eternal Spirit offered himself without spot to God, purge your conscience from dead works to serve the living God?" (Hebrews 9:14).

13. *Jesus was human in body. Before His resurrection, Jesus had the same kind of body (flesh and blood) that we have—capable of suffering, death, and decay and not able to inherit eternal life without a change.* "For in him dwelleth all the fulness of the Godhead bodily" (Colossians 2:9). "Wherefore when he cometh into the world, he saith, Sacrifice and offering thou wouldest not, but a body hast thou prepared me" (Hebrews 10:5). "Forasmuch then as the children are partakers of flesh and blood, he also himself likewise took part of the same; that through death he might destroy him that had the power of death, that is, the devil" (Hebrews 2:14). "Now this I say, brethren, that flesh and blood cannot inherit the kingdom of God; neither doth corruption inherit incorruption. Behold, I shew you a mystery; We shall not all sleep, but we shall all be changed" (I Corinthians 15:50-51).

14. *The resurrection of Christ gave Him a glorified body, which is not capable of suffering, death, or decay. Our resurrection will be the same as His and will give us a body like His.* In both cases, "resurrection" refers to the same process, so that Christ's resurrection made Him the "firstfruits" of the resurrec-

tion of believers. "But now is Christ risen from the dead, and become the firstfruits of them that slept. For since by man [Adam] came death, by man [Christ] came also the resurrection of the dead. For as in Adam all die, even so in Christ shall all be made alive. But every man in his own order: Christ the firstfruits; afterward they that are Christ's at his coming. . . . So also is the resurrection of the dead [Christ and us]. It is sown in corruption; it is raised in incorruption: it is sown in dishonour; it is raised in glory: it is sown in weakness; it is raised in power: it is sown a natural body; it is raised a spiritual body. There is a natural body, and there is a spiritual body. And so it is written, The first man Adam was made a living soul; the last Adam was made a quickening spirit" (I Corinthians 15:20-23, 42-45). "Knowing that Christ being raised from the dead dieth no more; death hath no more dominion over him" (Romans 6:9).

15. *Jesus is our kinsman redeemer, and to be this He had to become a human like us.* "And if a sojourner or stranger wax rich by thee, and thy brother that dwelleth by him wax poor, and sell himself unto the stranger or sojourner by thee, or to the stock of the stranger's family: after that he is sold he may be redeemed again; one of his brethren may redeem him: either his uncle, or his uncle's son, may redeem him, or any that is nigh of kin unto him of his family may redeem him; or if he be able, he may redeem himself" (Leviticus 25:47-49). "But when the fulness of the time was come, God sent forth his Son, made of a woman, made under the law, to redeem them that were under the law, that we might receive the adoption of sons" (Galatians 4:4-5). "For both he that sanctifieth and they who are sanctified

are all of one: for which cause he is not ashamed to call them brethren" (Hebrews 2:11).

Errors of Teaching the "Divine Flesh" of Christ

The doctrine known as the "divine flesh" of Christ says that the flesh of Jesus Christ had no biological or genetic relationship to other human beings, that Mary was not His biological mother, and that He did not have the same kind of humanity, albeit sinless, as Adam and Eve and their descendants. Here are the major problems with this doctrine:

1. *It contradicts many specific passages of Scripture*, as just discussed, at best interpreting them allegorically instead of literally.

2. *It undermines the truth of the Incarnation*—that God truly came in human flesh, that Jesus Christ was truly one of us with human identity while at the same time being God Himself. (See Matthew 1:21-23; John 1:1, 14; Colossians 2:9; I Timothy 3:16; I John 4:2.)

3. *It undermines the truth of the Atonement*—that Jesus Christ truly became our mediator as a human, became our kinsman redeemer, shed human blood for the remission of our sins, paid the penalty for our sins, and died in our place. (See Isaiah 53:4-6; I Corinthians 5:7; II Corinthians 5:21; I Timothy 2:5; Hebrews 2:9; 9:28; 10:10-17; I Peter 2:24.)

4. *It causes division in the church*, often by violation of ministerial ethics and often by undermining the assurance of salvation. In this regard, we need to follow the same ethical guidelines worldwide. (See Matthew 7:12.)

Forward, Summer 2001

CHAPTER 19

Christianity without the Cross?

A recent book alleges that Oneness Pentecostals teach Christianity without the Cross. Our response is that our salvation, from start to finish, is based on the atoning sacrifice of Jesus Christ.

We affirm the doctrines of the Cross, or the Atonement; salvation by grace through faith; and the new birth according to Acts 2:38. The doctrine of the Atonement says that the only way human beings can be saved is by the sacrifice of Jesus Christ on Calvary. His sinless blood is essential for remission of sins; His death is essential for our salvation.

The doctrine of grace says that salvation is a free gift of God that we cannot deserve but was purchased for us by Christ's death. The doctrine of faith says that we cannot receive the gift of salvation by our good works but only by trusting in Jesus Christ and relying upon His work for us. Moreover, faith in God's Word becomes real only as we act in faith, by obeying God's Word. The doctrine of the new birth tells us what happens when we receive God's grace and exercise saving faith. Specifically, under the new covenant, the application of God's grace and the expression of saving faith occur when we repent, receive water baptism in Jesus' name, and receive the gift of the Holy Ghost. These steps are not good works on our part, but they are God's gift to us and God's work in us as we respond to His Word by obedient faith.

Why should we expect to go to heaven? Because Jesus Christ died for our sins, was buried in the tomb, and rose again on the third day; and because we have applied His atoning death, burial, and resurrection to our lives by faith. In other words, we do not deserve to go to heaven because of what we have done, but we claim eternal life because we have personally believed and received what Jesus Christ has done for us.

Why, then, would anyone accuse us of denying the Cross? In a radio interview, the author of the book presented three summary points to support his position: (1) In an informal survey of about 200 Oneness ministers, 80 percent agreed that we don't preach about the Cross or don't preach about it enough. (2) Several years ago, a Oneness minister published a book that says we need to emphasize the Cross more than we do. (3) Our emphasis on Acts 2:38 undermines the message of the Cross.

The first two points are easily refuted, as they are merely anecdotal evidence, not statistically valid surveys. Indeed, they actually demonstrate that Oneness people believe in the importance of the Cross—so much so that they consistently express a desire for greater emphasis on the Cross. As an analogy, what would our ministers answer to the following questions: "Do you pray enough, or should you pray more than you do? Does your church evangelize as much as it should, or should it do more to win the lost?"

Possibly 80 percent or more would say that we should pray more and evangelize more. Would this mean we currently deny the importance of prayer and evangelism, or that we do not make prayer and evangelism a significant part of our lives? Of course not. More likely it would mean that we value prayer and evangelism so much that we are not satisfied with what we are currently doing.

The third point is the crux of the matter. No matter how much we might preach messages on Calvary, the Cross, and the blood of Jesus, the author would still say we deny the Cross because he is opposed to our new-birth message. In other words, he erroneously thinks that anyone who preaches the necessity of repentance, water baptism, and the Holy Ghost baptism is denying the Cross. But actually this message establishes the Cross, because it is the Cross that has purchased these benefits for us.

The book spends much of its time asserting that many figures in Oneness Pentecostal history did not believe in the necessity of Acts 2:38 for New Testament salvation, and it claims that we try to hide this evidence. (Interestingly, the author does some hiding of his own: He does not disclose that he once attended a United Pentecostal Church but left over doctrinal issues long before he began this project. He tries to present his findings as the outcome of neutral, objective, scholarly research instead of a predetermined agenda.) In my book *A History of Christian Doctrine, Volume 3: The Twentieth Century*, I documented that the overwhelming majority of Oneness Pentecostals—probably 85 to 90 percent— historically agreed that Acts 2:38 is the new birth. Our own publications forthrightly acknowledge that there were some differences of opinion on this subject but explain that most ministers decided to unite around the message of Acts 2:38, thus forming the United Pentecostal Church International (UPCI).

The two predecessor organizations of the UPCI were the Pentecostal Assemblies of Jesus Christ (PAJC) and the Pentecostal Church Incorporated (PCI). Everyone acknowledges that very few in the PAJC believed that the new birth occurred before the complete application of Acts 2:38, and the analysis in chapter 4 of my book has shown that this was a minority view even in the PCI. At the merger in 1945, the PCI directory listed 175 churches and the PAJC directory listed 346. Using these statistics, even if half the PCI pastors held this position, only 17 percent of the merged body would have done so. If one-third of PCI pastors held this position, only 11 percent of the merged body would have done so. In short, we conclude that at least 85 percent of the merged body held that the full Acts 2:38 experience was essential to salvation.

It is also interesting that the author relied primarily on anecdotal and secondhand evidence to demonstrate the beliefs of some leaders, while virtually ignoring their own statements. He also relied heavily on people who have left our ranks over the years for various reasons and on people who are outside the mainstream of our movement. While some information gleaned by such interviews is interesting, its significance can only be determined by a careful consideration of the sources.

For instance, to assert that a leader was opposed to the new-birth message, he might quote the opinion of a minister who has left the UPCI over this very issue, who naturally seeks as much support as possible. Then as corroboration, the author might interview an extremely strict minister who thinks the UPCI is too tolerant and who would therefore identify the same leader as a compromiser. Thus, from the mouths of two witnesses from the margins, the leader might be characterized contrary to his own statements, actions, and place in our movement.

The real issue is this: Does the New Testament teach that everyone should repent, be baptized in the name of Jesus Christ, and receive the gift of the Holy Ghost with the initial sign of speaking in tongues? The answer is unequivocally yes. This experience is God's plan for us and God's gift to us. Thus, by definition, it comes from God's grace and was purchased by the Atonement. It is the New Testament experience of full salvation.

In sum, we would do well to evaluate our thinking, writing, singing, preaching, and teaching to make sure that we give supreme attention to redemption through the blood of Jesus and salvation through the Cross of Christ. The Incarnation and Atonement must always be our fundamental message; the experience of salvation must rest on that foundation. First and foremost, we must preach Jesus Christ and Him crucified. When we do, then we will also proclaim the wonderful experience of the new birth and the new life of holiness, which are purchased for us by the Cross. It is the blood of Jesus Christ that touches our minds when we first hear the gospel, supersedes the influence of sin in repentance, washes away our sins in water baptism, opens our hearts to receive the Holy Ghost, gives us power to live a holy life pleasing to God, and enables us to walk with the Lord every day.

Forward, September-October 2004, with one paragraph from July-August 2004

CHAPTER 20

Discussion between Trinitarian and Oneness Pentecostals

For historical, theological, and practical reasons, it is important for Trinitarian and Oneness Pentecostals to communicate with each other and to develop a greater understanding of one another's beliefs. When both groups were small and rejected by mainline society and religion, it was relatively easy for them to remain isolated from the world and from each other. Today, however, both groups have experienced such growth and acceptance that they need to consider how to relate to each other as well as to the world at large.

The growth of Pentecostals as a whole is well documented, but Trinitarian Pentecostals are just now beginning to acknowledge the growth of the Oneness movement. In June 1997, *Charisma* magazine reported 17 million Oneness believers.[1] The most thorough study of this subject, presented as a master's thesis for Wheaton College in 1998, documented approximately 20 million Oneness Pentecostals worldwide.[2]

Trinitarian Pentecostals typically have misconceptions about Oneness Pentecostal beliefs and practices. As a result, misinformation is commonly disseminated. For example, a 1997 study of Pentecostals erroneously states that in the view of Oneness pioneer Frank Ewart "baptism in the Holy Spirit . . . [was] received only in the immersion rite and only if administered in the name of Jesus."[3] It further claims that "many" independent Jesus Name congregations "practice such oddities as snake-handling and free love."[4] No source is given for either assertion, and there is no reason to believe that the cited "oddities" are any more prevalent among Oneness churches than Trinitarian churches. Similarly, a 1990 work erroneously says that Oneness Pentecostals consider water baptism to be "valid only when the newly baptized spoke in other tongues."[5]

Oneness Pentecostals do not seek the approval of Trinitarians, nor would they necessarily wish to participate in various ecumenical activities. They would, however, appreciate a respectful, fair, and accurate treatment of their historical and present significance to the Pentecostal movement and to Christianity generally, and they would welcome discussion.

Theologically, three factors have blocked significant discussion between Trinitarian and Oneness Pentecostals: (1) the doctrine of the Oneness of God, ever since the adoption of an explicitly Trinitarian statement of faith by the Assemblies of God in 1916, (2) the apostolic soteriology of Oneness Pentecostals, and (3) the conservative holiness practices espoused by most Oneness Pentecostals in contrast to most Trinitarian Pentecostals today.

With regard to the doctrine of God, we must remember that the Assemblies of God was founded on the basis that there would be no creed but the Bible, that the One-

ness movement began about the same time as the formation of the Assemblies of God, and that many early
Pentecostal leaders embraced the Oneness doctrine,
including workers under Charles Parham and at the
Azusa Street Mission. The Oneness people in 1916
argued for continued fellowship but were voted out.

Oneness believers are not likely to modify their core
beliefs on the Godhead, but discussion could help to dis-
pel misconceptions, eliminate false differences, and
clarify true differences. Perhaps it could lead to a greater
appreciation for insights offered by Oneness Pentecostals, some of which have been suggested in scholarly
terms by mainstream theologians.[6]

On the doctrine of salvation, the Fundamental Doctrine of the United Pentecostal Church International
(UPCI), the largest Oneness Pentecostal body, states:

> The basic and fundamental doctrine of this
> organization shall be the Bible standard of full
> salvation, which is repentance, baptism in water
> by immersion in the name of the Lord Jesus
> Christ for the remission of sins, and the baptism
> of the Holy Ghost with the initial sign of speaking
> with other tongues as the Spirit gives utterance.
>
> We shall endeavor to keep the unity of the
> Spirit until we all come into the unity of the faith,
> at the same time admonishing all brethren that
> they shall not contend for their different views to
> the disunity of the body.[7]

Oneness Pentecostals indeed believe that they have a
more complete understanding of "the Bible standard of

full salvation," but from the beginning they acknowledged the genuine spiritual experiences of other Pentecostals and non-Pentecostals. They spoke of a progressive experience of salvation as people walked in the light of the gospel, and they associated the fullness of salvation with the complete apostolic experience. In this regard, they followed the lead of the earliest Pentecostals.

The concept of "full salvation" appears in the writings of John Wesley and other Wesleyan and Holiness authors. Early Pentecostals applied the terms "full salvation" and "full gospel" to the baptism of the Holy Spirit.

The second paragraph of the Fundamental Doctrine of the UPCI is based on Ephesians 4:3, 13. Many early Pentecostals made a similar appeal to maintain "the unity of the Spirit until we all come into the unity of the faith." In 1913 this phrase appeared in the writings of Frank Ewart, D. W. Kerr, and Andrew Urshan, and on the masthead of *The Christian Evangel*.[8] In 1914 it appeared in the original constitution of the Assemblies of God.[9]

The first paragraph of the Fundamental Doctrine of the UPCI is based on Acts 2:38. Charles Parham wrote in 1902 that God drew his attention to the necessity of obeying Acts 2:38, and for a time he baptized in the name of Jesus Christ.[10] Many Pentecostal pioneers were baptized in the name of Jesus Christ, including chroniclers of the movement and founders of the Assemblies of God, the Pentecostal Assemblies of Canada, and the International Church of the Foursquare Gospel.[11] Parham also taught that to be in the church, the bride, the body of Christ, and the Rapture, one must be baptized with the Holy Spirit.[12] A few years later, William Durham (died

1912) "elevated Acts 2:38 to the normative pattern for Pentecostal belief and practice."[13]

In recent years, a number of evangelical and charismatic theologians have identified Acts 2:38 as the paradigm for New Testament salvation, including Leighton Ford, David Pawson, Kilian McDonnell, and George Montague.[14]

Discussion on this matter could be mutually enlightening. As one example, both Trinitarian and Oneness Pentecostals proclaim the importance of the baptism of the Holy Spirit. Among Trinitarian Pentecostals, however, only about 35 percent of members have received this experience.[15] In Oneness Pentecostal circles the percentage is far higher. In the church I founded in 1992 in Austin, Texas, about 90 percent of all those age ten and above have been baptized with the Holy Spirit, and most of the rest are relatively new to the church. It would be interesting to explore the reasons behind this significant difference.

On the practice of holiness, the potential for interaction on the grass-roots level becomes increasingly difficult due to the changing lifestyle of Trinitarian Pentecostals. In this regard, the Trinitarians, by and large, have changed, while the Oneness believers have consciously sought to maintain the holiness lifestyle that Pentecostals embraced from the beginning. Common ground diminishes when Trinitarian Pentecostals begin smoking, drinking socially, and wearing heavy ornamentation.[16]

It is common for Trinitarian Pentecostals and especially charismatics to deride Oneness Pentecostals for their conservative stance on such issues. In 1997 *Charisma* accused Oneness Pentecostals of legalism, elitism, mean-spiritedness, hypocrisy, judgmentalism, and spiritual pride, apparently with no awareness of the irony involved in judging them harshly based on anonymous or disgruntled sources.[17] A greater understanding and appreciation for our mutual Holiness-Pentecostal heritage would bring perspective on this subject.

To this point, the Society for Pentecostal Studies has served as the primary forum for theological interaction between Trinitarian and Oneness Pentecostals. Practically speaking, further discussion would have to come at the initiation of Trinitarians. Ideally, it would involve mainstream representatives of the Oneness movement. Some years ago, Nathaniel Urshan, then general superintendent of the UPCI, proposed such a discussion in a letter to the general superintendent of the Assemblies of God.

On a personal level, it is easy for Trinitarian and Oneness Pentecostals to find much common ground and to feel a kindred spirit. Worship, prayer, and preaching can be points of identity. When I have attended various evangelical functions, I have observed Trinitarian Pentecostals muting their distinctive beliefs and worship styles, even when they composed a majority, in order to attain the least common denominator required for ecumenism. Yet when I have had the liberty to interact with them on a personal level or in Pentecostal-style worship, it seems that we Pentecostals have more in common with each other than with evangelicals generally or with people in mainline denominations.

For instance, one Trinitarian Pentecostal interviewed me as part of his research for a master's thesis. His premise was that Oneness Pentecostals are a heretical cult who preach another gospel and worship a different

Jesus. I invited him to attend Sunday services at our church and to have social interaction with our people. When I asked him to stand and greet the congregation, he gave thanks that we worship the same Lord. His thesis still argues that the Oneness doctrine is erroneous, but it no longer accuses Oneness Pentecostals of worshiping a different Jesus.

Perhaps we could all benefit from a discussion in the context of classical Pentecostal prayer, worship, and Bible study.

Notes

[1] J. Lee Grady, "The Other Pentecostals," *Charisma*, June 1997, 63.

[2] Talmadge L. French, "Oneness Pentecostalism in Global Perspective: The Worldwide Growth and Organizational Expansion of the Oneness Pentecostal Movement in Historical and Theological Context" (master's thesis, Wheaton College Graduate School, 1998).

[3] Vinson Synan, *The Holiness-Pentecostal Tradition* (Grand Rapids: Eerdmans, 1997), 157.

[4] Ibid., 162.

[5] Vinson Synan, "An Equal Opportunity Movement," chap. 3 in Harold B. Smith, ed., *Pentecostals from the Inside Out* (Wheaton, Ill.: Victor Books, 1990), 45.

[6] See, for example, quotations from Oscar Cullmann, James Dunn, and Frank Stagg in David Bernard, "The Word Became Flesh: Oneness Pentecostal Perspectives on the Incarnation" (paper presented at the annual meeting of the Society for Pentecostal Studies, Springfield, Mo., March 1999).

[7] *Manual* (Hazelwood, Mo.: United Pentecostal Church International, 1998), 22. These two paragraphs compose a section of the UPCI's Articles of Faith entitled "Fundamental Doctrine." It appears every month in the *Pentecostal Herald*, the official organ of the UPCI.

[8] David Reed, "The 'New Issue' of 1914: New Revelation or Historical Development?" (paper presented at the annual meeting of the Society for Pentecostal Studies, Wheaton, Ill., November 1994), 8.

[9]*Combined Minutes of the General Council of the Assemblies of God, 1914-17*, 4-5.

[10]Charles Parham, *A Voice Crying in the Wilderness* (Baxter Springs, KS: Apostolic Faith Bible College, 1902), 21, 23-24. Howard Goss testified that Parham baptized him in the name of Jesus Christ in 1903. Fred Foster, *Their Story: 20th Century Pentecostals* (Hazelwood, Mo.: Word Aflame Press, 1975), 98, 121.

[11]See Walter Hollenweger, *The Pentecostals* (Peabody, Mass.: Hendrickson, 1972), 32, 43 n. 21. Examples are A. H. Argue, Frank Bartleman, E. N. Bell, Howard Goss, B. F. Lawrence, R. E. McAlister, Aimee Semple McPherson, D. C. O. Opperman, and H. G. Rodgers.

[12]Parham, 27, 31, 35.

[13]Reed, 22.

[14]Leighton Ford, "The 'Finger of God' in Evangelism," in J. I. Packer and Paul Fromer, eds., *The Best in Theology, Vol. 1* (Carol Stream, IL: Christianity Today, 1987), 292-93; J. David Pawson, *The Normal Christian Birth* (London: Hodder & Stoughton, 1989), 13, 143-46; Kilian McDonnell and George Montague, eds., *Fanning the Flame* (Collegeville, Minn.: The Liturgical Press, 1991), 14.

[15]D. B. Barrett, "Statistics Global," in Stanley M. Burgess, Gary B. McGee, and Patrick Alexander, eds., *Dictionary of Pentecostal and Charismatic Movements* (Grand Rapids: Zondervan, 1988), 820.

[16]In recent years the International Pentecostal Holiness Church officially abandoned its historic stand on these matters.

[17]Grady, 64-65.

Paper presented in a panel discussion at the annual meeting of the Society for Pentecostal Studies, Evangel University, Springfield, MO, March 11-13, 1999.

CHAPTER 21

Response to Robert Morey

The Trinity: Evidences and Issues (1996)
Chapter 22: "Modalism"

In Chapter 22 of this book, Robert Morey attacks ancient modalism and modern Oneness Pentecostalism, often interchanging the two, and he quotes frequently from my book *The Oneness of God* in the course of his refutation. The points he raises have been adequately discussed in my books *The Oneness of God (OG)* (1983), *The Oneness View of Jesus Christ (OVJC)* (1994), and *In the Name of Jesus (INJ)* (1992). To conserve time and space, I will not answer each point individually, but I will identify seven major problems with his analysis and then respond to his nine points in conclusion.

Problems with the Analysis of the Oneness Doctrine

1. *Morey never accurately states the Oneness position.* He never defines the doctrine of Oneness or explains how it treats subjects such as the Father, Son, and Holy Spirit. Consequently, the reader is left with a confused, piecemeal, straw-man presentation.

2. *Morey misunderstands and misrepresents key*

tenets of the Oneness position. Here are examples. (a) Morey asserts that the Oneness doctrine hides God behind masks, but Oneness proponents never speak in this way. To the contrary, the central teaching of Oneness is that God has *revealed* Himself in the person of Jesus Christ. (b) Morey falsely claims that instead of saying "Jesus is the Father," most Oneness people say "The Father is Jesus" and believe in "Jesus only." Oneness believers say that Jesus is the incarnation of the Father, but they do not believe the eternal Spirit is limited in time or space to the human body of Jesus. (See *OG*, 66; *OVJC*, 141.) Moreover, they hold that Jesus is an authentic human being in every way (except for sin), not merely a "nature" as Morey indicates. (c) Morey emphasizes that the roles of Father, Son, and Holy Spirit are distinct in the plan of salvation. This is exactly what Oneness people teach; however, they do not see these three roles as requiring three self-conscious persons. (See *OVJC*, 16.) (d) Morey emphasizes that Oneness believers have a new "revelation," whereas Oneness believers expressly repudiate the idea of extrabiblical revelation and instead simply believe in the illumination of Scripture by the Holy Spirit. (See *OG*, 66.) (e) Morey fails to understand that the Oneness doctrine recognizes a distinction between the eternal God and the true humanity in which God manifested Himself—not a plurality of persons but a distinction between Spirit and flesh.

3. *Morey falsely associates Oneness believers with ancient modalists, the Watchtower (Jehovah's Witnesses), Gnosticism, Swedenborgianism, Arianism, and Platonism.* There is no connection historically with any of these groups. Neither is there any connection doctri-

nally with most of them. It is true that the ancient modalists apparently had the same basic concept of God, but Morey resurrects ancient accusations against them and then imputes these to modern Oneness believers. For example, the ancient modalists allegedly spoke of God as acting with masks, so Oneness believers are guilty of the same thing. This method of argumentation is faulty, however. If Morey wishes to argue against Oneness believers, he should cite their own position and respond to it. Likewise, he tries to associate the alleged occultism of Swedenborg with Oneness believers simply because Swedenborg had a concept of one God, even though my book expressly repudiates the false ideas of Swedenborg (*OG*, 243). Morey's tactic here would be equivalent to my associating trinitarianism with Mormonism because both believe that the Father, Son, and Holy Spirit are three persons, or imputing the subordinationistic beliefs of Tertullian (whom Morey does cite with approval) to Morey himself.

4. *Morey misunderstands the purpose of my book.* He assumes that it was written merely to oppose trinitarianism and specifically against his views. Actually it was written to teach the biblical doctrine of God, starting with the Scriptures and building correct concepts. Thus he accuses me of wasting much space to establish monotheism and the deity of Christ when trinitarians already believe both. To the extent that trinitarians accept these truths, well and good! I want to establish these scriptural truths for everyone, and certainly there are many people, including Jehovah's Witnesses and Mormons, who need to be convinced of these principles.

5. *Morey misstates my position on a number of points.* For example, he accuses me of opposing the

doctrine of the trinity simply because its defining terminology is not found in Scripture. Actually, I say that the use of nonbiblical terminology itself is not fatal, but it does give rise to closer examination. (See *OG*, 287.) Then I explain that we must reject trinitarianism because the concepts are not found in Scripture. *All* the defining terms were borrowed from philosophy, and they do not express scriptural concepts. Morey also says that I reject the doctrine of the trinity because it is a mystery while accepting other things that transcend human reason. Actually, I simply pointed out that the Bible never speaks of number, plurality, or persons in the Godhead as a mystery; it only speaks of the Incarnation as a mystery. (See *OG*, 65.) In both cases, my argument is an appeal to the Bible, not an *a priori* rejection of a doctrine because of some philosophical deficiency.

6. *Morey accuses me of twenty-six logical fallacies because of an alleged confusion between the "ontological Trinity" and the "economical Trinity," but this point only makes sense if one presupposes the trinity.* Here he is guilty of circular reasoning. Where is the proof of the ontological (eternal) trinity? If we use the so-called economical (temporal) trinity, or a trinity of manifestations, to prove the ontological trinity, then we must use it to prove the nature of the ontological trinity. For example, if the distinction between the Father and Son in the Incarnation, such as we see in the prayers of Christ, proves that there is an eternal distinction of persons between Father and Son, then the Father is eternally superior and the Son is eternally inferior. If the Son's need of prayer relates only to the flesh, then the situation teaches nothing about the eternal nature of God.

7. *Morey devalues the saving name of Jesus,*
whereas Acts 4:10-12 identifies it as the only saving
name. Morey asserts that, according to Greek scholars,
the name in Philippians 2:9-11 is not "Jesus" but "Lord,"
but many Greek scholars emphasize the significance of
the name "Jesus" here. (See *INJ*, 51-52; *OVJC*, 49-50.)
For example, the most widely respected Greek-English
lexicon (that of Bauer, Arndt, Gingrich, and Danker) says
that, according to Philippians 2:10-11, "when the name
of Jesus is mentioned" every knee will bow and every
tongue will confess that Jesus Christ is Lord. While this
passage does identify Jesus as Lord, the point is not that
everyone will one day acknowledge a Lord, but that
everyone will specifically acknowledge *Jesus*—the
unique Jesus Christ of Nazareth—as Lord.

Reponse to "The Arguments against Modalism"

1. *Argument: Modalism has roots in Platonism.*
Response: Oneness theology has its roots in the Bible,
beginning with Old Testament Judaism. It has no roots in
Platonism. Would Morey argue that the Jews got their
monotheism from Plato?

2. *Argument: Oneness reasoning is circular and*
logically fallacious. Response: See point 6 above. Oneness reasoning is not circular. It starts with the
definitions of "God," "one God," "Lord," and so on from
the Old Testament and maintains them consistently as we
study the revelation of Jesus in the New Testament. Thus,
when the New Testament speaks of Jesus as God, it
means the one, undivided God of the Old Testament in all
His fullness. It is trinitarian reasoning that is circular. For
example, the sole distinctions among the three persons

of the trinity are that the Father is unbegotten, the Son is begotten, and the Holy Spirit is proceeding. Yet when one asks what these three properties mean, the answer is that they are a mystery. All trinitarians can say is that they are the qualities which make each person unique and distinct.

3. *Argument: Oneness devalues the significance of Father, Son, and Holy Spirit in Scripture.* Response: We recognize the importance and special character of God's three supreme manifestations as Father, Son, and Holy Spirit. (See, for example, *OVJC*, 141.) Indeed, we understand that God's work as Father, Son, and Spirit was necessary to implement the plan of salvation. The Son had to be born to identify with us, take our place, shed atoning blood, and die for our sins. For the sinless Son to be born, God had to be the Father. For this historic work of salvation to be applied to our hearts today, God must operate in our lives as the Holy Spirit. However, we do not regard these roles as requiring three self-conscious persons.

4. *Argument: Oneness interpretation ignores Hebrew grammatical usage in the Old Testament that demonstrates the trinity, such as plural pronouns and verbs used for God.* Response: Our explanations are convincing to the people to whom the Old Testament was originally given and who read it in its original language—namely, the Jews, ancient and modern. There is no evidence that the Old Testament Jews believed in a trinity. The use of a few plural words for God pales in significance to the thousands of singular words so used, and there are good reasons for the plural construction that do not involve a trinity. (See *OG*, 146-52.)

5. *Argument: Oneness interpretation ignores Greek grammatical usage in the New Testament that demonstrates the trinity, such as the Granville Sharp rule, which, when applied to Matthew 28:19, shows that Father, Son, and Holy Spirit are "separate Persons."* Response: The Granville Sharp rule of Greek grammar says, in part, that when two or more nouns are listed and separated by *kai* ("and") and each noun has the definite article ("the") in front of it, then the nouns refer to different persons, places, or things. As applied to Matthew 28:19, this rule simply identifies the Father, Son, and Holy Spirit as distinct in some way, which Oneness believers acknowledge. They are distinct manifestations or roles in our salvation, but all are fulfilled in, and revealed through, Jesus—in one name, not three names. To say that a grammatical rule requires them to be three "separate Persons" is to veer into theological interpretation. No mere rule of grammar can force three different nouns to be regarded as separate divine persons that are coequal, coeternal, and cosubstantial. Moreover, here Morey deviates from trinitarian orthodoxy, which affirms "distinct" persons but denies "separate" persons as tritheism.

6. *Argument: In John 8, Jesus said that both He and the Father were witnesses, thus requiring them to be two persons.* Response: In John 8, Jesus pointed out that both He as a man and His Father (the eternal God) bore witness to the Incarnation. This statement does not require two divine persons, but it simply underscores the truth that Jesus was an authentic human being in every way except for sin. In every way that we could speak of ourselves in relationship to God, Jesus could so speak of

139

Himself, except that He did not need to repent or be born again. As a man speaking to His hearers, He could verify His identity to them, but the invisible Spirit of God could independently verify the Incarnation by moving upon sincere seekers of truth.

7. *Argument: The Bible describes Jesus as sitting at the right hand of God, God as sending the Son, and the Son as offering Himself to God, all of which require two persons.* Response: The "right hand of God" is fully explained as symbolic of power and authority. (See *OG*, 200-6; *OVJC*, 119-27.) Prominent trinitarians such as Martin Luther and F. F. Bruce have agreed that this phrase is symbolic and does not speak of two literal bodies sitting next to each other. Moreover, one God can easily perform the multiple works mentioned here without compromising His essential oneness. The eternal God can cause a Son to be conceived, can incarnate Himself in the Son, and can send the Son from the womb of a virgin into the world on a mission to save lost humanity. Moreover, Jesus Christ is the sacrificial lamb, the blood of the sacrifice, the high priest who offers the sacrifice, the veil through which the high priest passes, and the heavenly judge who accepts the sacrifice. (See John 1:29; 5:22; Hebrews 9:11-12; 10:19-21.) He is David's son and David's Lord (Matthew 22:42-45), the root and offspring of David (Revelation 22:16), the builder of the house and the son in the house (Hebrews 3:1-6).

8. *Argument: The New Testament uses plural references for Father, Son, and Holy Spirit, thus requiring a trinity.* Response: The Oneness doctrine *requires* plural references regarding the Son and the

Father. There is an important distinction between God and man, the Spirit and the flesh. However, this is not a distinction within the Godhead, but a distinction between the eternal, transcendent Spirit and the human identity in which God manifested Himself, as I Timothy 2:5 shows: "For there is one God, and one mediator between God and men, the man Christ Jesus." Moreover, there is a conceptual distinction between God in His transcendence and God as He works in human hearts. (See John 16:13; I Corinthians 2:10-12.) The Holy Spirit is not another person but is specifically God in action, God working in our world and in our lives. (See Genesis 1:1-2; Acts 2:4.) In John 14:16-18, "another Comforter" does not mean another person, but another relationship and another form—Jesus no longer dwelling *with* believers in the *flesh* but coming back to dwell *in* believers in *spirit*. (For examples and discussion of various plural uses, see *OVJC*, 26-27, 64-65, 105-9.)

9. *Argument: The Oneness doctrine makes God an unknowable entity hidden behind three masks.* Response: Morey misses the whole point of the Oneness message, completely misrepresenting its essence. Oneness does not teach an unknowable God, but trinitarians do, for they teach a mysterious trinity whose true identity and properties cannot be fathomed. Rather, Oneness teaches that the one God has come in the flesh, has become visible, has revealed His true character, power, authority, and presence—in the person of Jesus Christ. Jesus is not just *a* visible manifestation of God; He is *the* incarnation of God, the unique manifestation of God in flesh. He is indeed the invisible God made visible.

Our Creator became our Savior and has come to dwell

inside us as the Holy Spirit. We know Him fully as revealed in Jesus Christ, who is the true God. He is worthy of all worship, praise, and love forever and ever!

Unpublished response circulated upon request

CHAPTER 22

The Last Things

A study of Scripture reveals that we are living in the last days. The coming of our Lord Jesus Christ for His church is drawing near.

Consequently, it is no surprise that end-time prophecy is a subject of intense interest and speculation, especially in the new millennium. Different teachers have propounded a variety of prophetic scenarios, and some of them are quite sensational in their approach.

It is important to emphasize scriptural truths rather than personal opinions on this subject and at the same time to cultivate an awareness of the soon coming of the Lord. Several principles are important in helping us to maintain a balance in this area.

Guiding Principles

First, we must live by faith in Jesus Christ and not put our faith in a certain prophetic scheme. Some people are so adamant that the Lord will catch away the church before the Tribulation that they do not seem to prepare themselves for the possibility of trials, opposition, or persecution in this life. On the other hand, other people are equally adamant that the Lord will not catch away His church before the Tribulation, and so do not seem to cultivate an expectancy of His soon coming.

In both cases, the remedy is to emphasize that we walk by faith in Jesus. Whether we are right or wrong in our understanding of end-time events, we will be saved if we obey the gospel and continue in the faith. Regardless of the circumstances, we will find that God's grace is sufficient. If unexpected tribulation comes our way, we will not waver. If Christ comes before other expected events, we will be prepared. If our faith is in Jesus Christ, we will be ready no matter what the future holds.

Second, we must maintain genuine humility. It is the nature of prophecy that some things remain obscure or subject to different interpretations. In retrospect, it is amazing and awe inspiring to see the fulfillment of biblical prophecy, but when we look into the future there is always an element of the symbolic, the mysterious, and the unknown. While the Bible is absolutely true, we must acknowledge that we are not infallible in our interpretation of it. We may be wrong when we make specific predictions about the future based on a particular prophetic scenario.

Third, we must beware of excessive dogmatism. An understanding of end-time events is important and brings blessings to us, but it is not essential to salvation. Therefore, we must not contend for our views so much that we strain relationships with brethren of like precious faith. While it is good to have confidence in our beliefs, it is not necessary or even desirable to seek comprehensive knowledge and absolute certainty on matters that the Bible reveals only partially.

Fourth, we must uphold Christian ethics. It is wrong to emphasize certain prophetic views to the point that we hurt another believer or another church. It is wrong to encourage someone to change churches because of differences on such issues.

Fifth, we must practice Christian liberty. We need unity on the essentials of the faith, but we must allow for a diversity of views on end-time prophecy. It is wrong to condemn another believer or church for espousing different beliefs regarding a specific fulfillment or sequence of events. These issues must not become a test of fellowship or of salvation.

Essential Prophetic Teachings of Scripture

Of course, all those who believe that the Bible is the inerrant Word of God should unite in proclaiming its fundamental message. What are its essential teachings in the area of prophecy? What must we affirm on this subject if we are to uphold the authority of the Bible?

First, we must affirm the catching away of the saints, often called the Rapture. Paul wrote, "Behold, I shew you a mystery; We shall not all sleep, but we shall all be changed, in a moment, in the twinkling of an eye, at the last trump: for the trumpet shall sound, and the dead shall be raised incorruptible, and we shall be changed" (I Corinthians 15:51-52). "For the Lord himself shall descend from heaven with a shout, with the voice of the archangel, and with the trump of God: and the dead in Christ shall rise first: then we which are alive and remain shall be caught up together with them in the clouds, to meet the Lord in the air: and so shall we ever be with the Lord" (I Thessalonians 4:16-17).

145

Second, there will come upon the human race a time of unprecedented calamity and judgment, often called the Tribulation. Jesus explained that "the abomination of desolation" would take place in the Temple, and after that event "then shall be great tribulation, such as was not since the beginning of the world to this time, no, nor ever shall be. And except those days should be shortened, there should no flesh be saved" (Matthew 24:15, 21-22). It appears that Revelation 6-19 presents the events of this time. These chapters describe the rise of "the beast" or "man of sin" (II Thessalonians 2:3), often called the Antichrist, who will oppose God and seek to rule the world.

Third, Jesus Christ is coming back to earth again. When Jesus ascended to heaven, two angels told His disciples, "This same Jesus, which is taken up from you into heaven, shall so come in like manner as ye have seen him go into heaven" (Acts 1:11). He will come back to earth with all His saints (I Thessalonians 3:13). He will set foot upon the Mount of Olives, and He will destroy the armies of the beast (Zechariah 14; Revelation 19).

Fourth, when He returns to earth and defeats the beast, *Jesus will establish a kingdom on earth for a thousand years,* often called the Millennium. "Blessed and holy is he that hath part in the first resurrection: on such the second death hath no power, but they shall be priests of God and of Christ, and shall reign with him a thousand years" (Revelation 20:6). "And the LORD shall be king over all the earth: in that day shall there be one LORD, and his name one" (Zechariah 14:9).

Fifth, after Christ's reign of a thousand years and after one last rebellion against Him, *the final judgment will take place.* "And I saw a great white throne, and him that sat on it, from whose face the earth and the heaven fled away; and there was found no place for them. And I saw the dead, small and great, stand before God; and the books were opened: and another book was opened, which is the book of life: and the dead were judged out of those things which were written in the books, according to their works. And the sea gave up the dead which were in it; and death and hell delivered up the dead which were in them: and they were judged every man according to their works. And death and hell were cast into the lake of fire. This is the second death. And whosoever was not found written in the book of life was cast into the lake of fire" (Revelation 20:11-15).

Sixth, based on their response in this life to God's plan of salvation, *every human being will inherit either eternal life (salvation) or eternal death (damnation)*. Jesus explained, "He that heareth my word, and believeth on him that sent me, hath everlasting life, and shall not come into condemnation; but is passed from death unto life. Verily, verily, I say unto you, The hour is coming, and now is, when the dead shall hear the voice of the Son of God: and they that hear shall live. . . . Marvel not at this: for the hour is coming, in the which all that are in the graves shall hear his voice, and shall come forth; they that have done good, unto the resurrection of life; and they that have done evil, unto the resurrection of damnation" (John 5:24-25, 28-29).

Those who have become righteous by faith in Jesus Christ will live forever with glorified human bodies like His resurrected body (Philippians 3:21; I John 3:2). They will dwell with Him in a real place that He has prepared.

147

"In my Father's house are many mansions: if it were not so, I would have told you. I go to prepare a place for you. And if I go and prepare a place for you, I will come again, and receive you unto myself; that where I am, there ye may be also" (John 14:2-3).

The eternal abode of the saints is commonly called heaven and is also usually identified with "the holy city, new Jerusalem" (Revelation 21:2). In Scripture, "heaven" can refer to (a) earth's atmosphere; (b) outer space; or (c) the dwelling place of God and the angels, wherever it may be. (See Genesis 1:1, 8; 15:5; 28:12, 17; I Kings 8:30). The third meaning corresponds to the future home of the saints, for they will dwell in God's presence forever (Revelation 21:3-4, 22-27). While believers are already part of the invisible "kingdom of heaven" or "kingdom of God," meaning the rule of God in the hearts of His people, they yet await the future, visible, universal manifestation of the kingdom of God throughout eternity.

The unrighteous will be cast into "the lake of fire," also called hell. In Scripture, "hell" can refer to (a) the temporary abode of the souls of the dead as they await resurrection and judgment (Greek, *hades*); (b) the prison for some fallen angels (Greek, *tartarus*); or (c) the place of final judgment for the unrighteous (Greek, *gehenna*). (See Mark 9:43-48; Luke 16:22-23; Acts 2:31; II Peter 2:4.) The third meaning corresponds to the eternal destiny of the unrighteous. Jesus described it as a place of "outer darkness" and "everlasting fire," a place "where their worm dieth not, and the fire is not quenched" (Matthew 25:30, 41; Mark 9:44). Paul similarly explained that Jesus will come "in flaming fire taking vengeance on them that know not God, and that obey not the gospel of our Lord Jesus Christ: who shall be punished with everlasting destruction from the presence of the Lord, and from the glory of his power" (II Thessalonians 1:7-9).

Conclusion

What should be our focus as we contemplate these awesome and pertinent truths of Scripture? We must realize that "for yet a little while, and he that shall come will come, and will not tarry" (Hebrews 10:37). We must prepare now for the end-time events by making sure of our salvation. Jesus admonished, "Be ye also ready: for in such an hour as ye think not the Son of man cometh" (Matthew 24:44). Finally, let us heed the final words of Jesus recorded in Scripture, and let us respond as the apostle John did in Revelation 22:20: "He which testifieth these things saith, Surely I come quickly. Amen. Even so, come, Lord Jesus."

Pentecostal Herald, July 1998

MINISTRY

CHAPTER 23

Revival in the Time of Promise

But when the time of the promise drew nigh, which God had sworn to Abraham, the people grew and multiplied in Egypt (Acts 7:17).

We are living in the days of revival and church growth, as promised by Almighty God. And it is time to claim that promise!

The ancient Israelites had a promise of deliverance from Egypt. When it was God's time for them to become a mighty nation, they grew and multiplied.

On the Day of Pentecost, the apostle Peter preached that the time had come for the prophecy of Joel 2 to be fulfilled: "And it shall come to pass in the last days, saith God, I will pour out of my Spirit upon all flesh" (Acts 2:17). As they claimed this promise, the early church experienced dramatic revival and growth (Acts 2:41, 47; 6:7).

The Promise of Revival Today

If the last days began with Pentecost, then how much more are we living in the last days! If the apostles could claim this promise, how much more can we!

In the twentieth century, there was an unprecedented revival of the Holy Spirit. In 1900, no organized group proclaimed the baptism of the Holy Ghost with the initial evidence of speaking in tongues. But after a hundred years, over five hundred million people professed some type of Pentecostal or charismatic identity. Even though many of these people have not received the Holy Ghost, and most do not have the fullness of apostolic truth, yet the growth and acceptance of the Pentecostal movement has truly been miraculous. It has touched every country of the world and every denomination. If the Lord tarries for some years in the twenty-first century, we can see an equal revival of the name of Jesus, as well as a revival of true holiness.

I am thankful for what God has done, but I am not satisfied. There needs to be a holy dissatisfaction in our hearts. We thank God for our heritage, and we must not change our apostolic identity. But we must press forward to claim revival in the time of promise. Revival is the will of God, but it is not automatic. We must claim it by faith and work to see it become a reality.

A Personal Promise

Shortly after my wife and I started New Life Church in Austin in 1992, the Lord gave me a message from Acts 18:9-10. This message was originally for the apostle Paul when he went to Corinth, but the principle applies to us. Every pastor and home missionary needs to receive some personal promises from God.

The Lord told Paul, "Be not afraid, but speak, and hold not thy peace: for I am with thee, and no man shall set on thee to hurt thee: for I have much people in this city." If God could do this for Paul, He can do it for us!

God did not say there would be no opposition. In fact, His words indicated that there would be opposition. But He promised that no one would attack the apostle in such a way as to bring about the ultimate destruction of him or his work. In other words, we will be attacked, but we will not be defeated if we hold on to God's promise.

We have found this to be true in Austin. We came with assurance and promises from God. We made contacts, taught Bible studies, and visited people. We gathered a small group from various backgrounds, including those with some sort of Pentecostal or charismatic experience. But to my great disappointment, for six months we did not have one brand-new convert to repent, be baptized, and receive the Holy Ghost for the first time under our ministry. After six months, a young African-American woman repented in our living room after a home Bible study. We baptized her in a swimming pool, and when she came up, we laid hands on her. She began speaking in tongues as the Spirit gave utterance. We had our first breakthrough! But we only won a few more converts in the next six months.

After one year, I asked a nearby pastor, Tim Wallace from San Antonio, to preach some evangelistic services for us. He brought many of his congregation, so we were able to fill our little rented building. In one night, four people received the Holy Spirit. Two of them had come with his church, and one was a backslider in Austin from his church, but one was a first-time visitor from Austin. She is in our church today, along with her husband, mother, and brother. Her husband is our head usher and a church board member, and together they lead our singles' ministry.

In our second calendar year, twelve received the Holy Spirit. Slowly, we continued to experience revival and growth. We have had our ups and downs, but we have continued to move forward. Now we regularly see over one hundred people filled with the Holy Spirit each year through the ministry of our church.

In the process of time we have started eleven daughter works. One of them has been shut down, but three of them are now autonomous churches. Three have their own land and building, and we are in the process of obtaining land for two more. Our first work was a Spanish outreach, for at that time we had no Spanish-speaking United Pentecostal Church in Austin. We actually started it three times before we succeeded in establishing a permanent work.

In short, if we claim our promise, we will have revival. If we hold on to our promise through trials, setbacks, opposition, and attacks, we will be victorious. This principle holds true for an individual, a local church, and a district. Let's claim revival in the time of promise!

Claiming the Promise

How can we claim this promise?

First, we must restore the apostolic church, as found in Acts 2, including apostolic experience, doctrine, fellowship and unity, prayer and praise, and signs and wonders. In every local church we need to expect the miraculous—the operation of the gifts of the Spirit. If we will truly be apostolic in these five dimensions, the Lord will add "to the church daily such as should be saved" (Acts 2:47).

Second, we must evangelize everywhere. In Genesis 12, God called Abraham to come out of his homeland and his father's house and promised to make of him a great nation. In Genesis 13, after Abraham separated from his nephew Lot, God renewed the covenant with him. God told Abraham to look north, south, east, and west, and God would give him all the land he could see.

Although Abraham was the elder and the leader, he had allowed Lot the first choice of land. Lot had chosen the well-watered plains near the sinful city of Sodom, while Abraham was left with the barren hillsides. As it turned out, God's promise was much more valuable to him on the hills than in the plain. He could see much farther and could inherit much more.

Similarly, we sometimes make consecrations that seem disadvantageous to the world, but they actually lead to greater blessings. This is no time to compromise our identity. When we make a clear separation from the world and a clear commitment to God, He will give us great promises.

Furthermore, God told Abraham that He would give him all the land he would walk upon. In other words, if what he could see wasn't enough, he could start walking. He could claim land as far as he was willing to travel. Even so, today God wants to give us revival everywhere we are willing to go.

What counties and towns don't have a church? What cities are underevangelized? What neighborhoods are not being reached? What ethnic groups are underrepresented? What homes need a Bible study? Let us take the gospel everywhere and claim our promise of revival!

Third, we must evangelize everyone. Let's break down any barriers that would stop us from reaching every individual. Let's break traditional molds—not our doctrine or lifestyle but ways of thinking that can hinder us from evangelizing souls.

In Acts 13:1, we find Antioch, the missionary church, the church that was most effective in reaching the Gentiles. Among their leaders was Barnabas, a Levite from Cyprus, raised as a traditional Jew. Next was Simeon, called Niger, which means "black" in Latin. He must have had a dark complexion. He was probably an African from North Africa, where they spoke Latin instead of Greek. Another leader was Lucius of Cyrene, which is in North Africa. Then there was Manaen, who was brought up with King Herod. He was apparently of noble descent and high economic status. Finally, there was Saul of Tarsus, trained in the highest degree of theological education.

Notice the diversity: people from two continents, Jew and Gentile, different cultures, different races, different colors, different educational backgrounds, different economic classes. That was the model for apostolic church leadership.

We must break down barriers in the church and in leadership in order to reach everyone. If we want end-time revival, we must consider the end-time harvest. Some of our greatest revivals will be among Spanish-speaking people and among African-Americans. We must not limit the harvest!

According to James 2:9, prejudice is not merely rude or bad; it is a sin. Therefore, we must strive to reach a diversity of people. What can we do to foster revival among different groups of people?

Is it a coincidence that believers were first called Christians at Antioch? (See Acts 11:26.) To the outside world, the early Christians were just another sect of Jews. But when Jews and Gentiles joined together in the Antioch church, even to the extent of sharing leadership, people began to realize that the Christians were a new group. As Jesus said, "By this shall all men know that ye are my disciples, if ye have love one to another" (John 13:35). Apparently, the diversity of the revival caused the world to understand who Christians were. The world needs to see the same type of revival today.

We need to reach those no one else is reaching. We need to reach the "down and outers"—the homeless, the residents of halfway houses, those addicted to drugs. We also need to reach the "up and outers"—the professionals, the educated, the socially successful. In our church, we have seen agnostics, Buddhists, Muslims, Jehovah's Witnesses, and Mormons receive the Holy Spirit, as well as Catholics and Protestants.

Don't be intimidated by the categories of race, social status, or creed. Be yourself, and be real. Show people that you love them, want to learn about them, and will accept them into the church and ultimately into the leadership of the church. Get self out of the way, and let the love of God flow through you.

Seeing the Promise Fulfilled Personally

When I was a small child, my parents started a home missions church in Louisiana, and then they became the pioneer missionaries of the United Pentecostal Church of Korea. From them I learned the importance of trying to reach everyone everywhere by all means. My father typically led five services on Sunday. For a time, he pastored one church while my mother pastored another.

In addition, they established a ministry for American soldiers. In the 1960s in Seoul, blacks, whites, and Asians joined together for worship in the afternoon English service. After some African-American soldiers were baptized in Jesus' name, they hired an interpreter and started a church near their army base. God used a white missionary and black soldiers to start a Korean church. That is the way the church is supposed to work!

When my sister Karen was about ten years old, she became very successful at bringing her friends to church. We packed over twenty children in our Land Rover on Sunday. Finally, my father decided to organize a Sunday school in our garage, and from that effort a new church began in our neighborhood.

When the Korean work was ready for national leadership, my parents returned to America. Eventually, they started a home missions church in south Louisiana. It was difficult to watch them work on secular jobs after over twenty-five years of full-time ministry. But they did what they had to do to start a church. Not only did they establish that church, but they won some Spanish-speaking people and started a Spanish-speaking church—the first one in Louisiana to acquire its own building. My dad does not speak Spanish, but he never considered that he could not start a Spanish church. Now, at age seventy-five, he is the senior pastor of the Spanish-speaking church and the outreach director of the English-speaking church, both of which have their own pastors.

In the beginning of our church in Austin, I put an advertisement in the paper. Only one person answered—a seventy-six-year-old Hispanic woman who was an invalid and who spoke broken English. She wanted me to visit her home and pray for her. At first, I thought this would be a wasted effort. What were the chances of converting someone in her situation, especially considering the barriers of language and culture? But she was the only one who had responded, so I decided to walk through the door that God had opened.

My wife and I began to visit her, occasionally bringing groceries or picking up medicine. My wife taught her a Bible study of four simple lessons. At the end, she said, "No one has ever told me that Jesus died for me. I'm an old woman. Do you think I could be forgiven of all the sins of my whole life?"

My wife answered, "Yes, you can," and explained to her again about repentance and water baptism in Jesus' name. I baptized her in her bathtub in the name of Jesus. I wanted to make sure she understood clearly, so I learned enough Spanish to say, "En el nombre del Señor Jesucristo." She came up out of the water with her sins washed away and a happy countenance. A few days later, God filled her with the Spirit as she prayed in her home.

My older son, Jonathan, won three of his high school classmates to the Lord. He would invite them to spend the night on Saturday so they could attend service on Sunday morning. He would bring them home from school to eat dinner on Wednesday so they could attend Bible study that night.

We treated them like part of the family, and they began calling my wife and me Mom and Dad. One time at church I announced, "I have my three natural-born kids here, and I also have my three adopted kids." I thought I had better explain, so I added, "Well, they're not really my kids; I'm just their honorary dad." That week I received a card in the mail from one of them, who doesn't have a father. The card said simply, "You are not just my honorary dad."

My second son, Daniel, has brought more visitors to the church than the rest of the family combined. This year he came up with a plan and sold it to the family. As a result, we have an exchange student from Korea living in our home, and we are praying for God to work in his life.

This past year my daughter, Lindsey, age thirteen, has brought two of her classmates to church, as often as their parents would allow. One of them has received the Holy Spirit.

Conclusion

Testimonies such as these are common to our movement. Everyone can claim the promise of revival personally.

Let's go everywhere with the apostolic message, walk through every open door, and overcome every barrier to reach everyone we can. We need laborers for every area of the harvest, both in the local church and beyond the local church. Let's claim our revival! It's our time of promise!

Pentecostal Herald, June 2006; *South Texas Vision*, January-February 2006 and March-April 2006. Excerpted from a message at the General Conference of the United Pentecostal Church International on September 30, 2005, in Richmond, Virginia.

CHAPTER 24

The Confirming Power of the Gospel

"Take this car to the garage and search it!" the captain of the communist border guard ordered his subordinate. As Samuel Balca, our representative to Eastern Europe, deciphered the words and relayed their meaning to us, our hearts sank.

We immediately thought of the Bulgarian manuscript entitled "The Oneness of God" that was lying on the back dash of our car. We tried not to imagine what would happen when the guard found it. Would we be detained and interrogated or merely denied entrance to the country? Either way, our careful plans would be defeated.

Samuel Balca, my wife, and I were seeking to enter Bulgaria, which in 1988 was a strictly controlled communist country. We had been invited by an underground Pentecostal group to teach a doctrinal seminar on the oneness of God and the new birth, and we were bringing Oneness literature for underground copying and distribution. It was an exciting opportunity, for never before had United Pentecostal ministers preached, taught, or distributed literature in that country. At the same time, as the border search indicated, we faced many potential difficulties.

For example, we later learned that the pastor who invited us had previously been jailed and exiled and his wife had been beaten. Shortly before our visit, a trinitarian minister from America had also been beaten when three men broke into his hotel room at night. And the very week of our visit, the authorities had discovered where the believers were gathering for worship and threatened to burn down the house.

Before making the trip I had prayed, "God, if You open this door, I will go through it. If it is not Your will for us to go at this time, please let us know. If I go in Your will, then I will trust You, and regardless of what happens, I know that You will control the situation and that You will confirm Your Word."

Now it was time for me to believe those words and rely upon that prayer. We drove to the garage that was specially built for intense searches. The guard searched under the car, under the hood, inside the car from front to back, and through all of our luggage. He felt the paneling and carpeting to see if anything was concealed beneath them. Tools were available for ripping or dismantling anything that seemed suspicious. The guard was professionally trained to find what we had, and he probably took extra care since his superior singled us out for special treatment.

I had an English-language *National Geographic* in my luggage, and the guard became particularly suspicious of it. I explained carefully that I brought it for recreational reading only. I wondered, If he is so upset over an English magazine that has nothing to say about communism, Bulgaria, religion, or anything the government would object to, what is going to happen when he finds the Bulgarian manuscript that has Scripture on every page?

The manuscript was lying on the back dash, covered only by a wrapped gift package. We did not try to conceal it, for as tourists we had hoped to cross the border without a search. Moreover, we knew that a search would certainly uncover the manuscript no matter how carefully it was hidden, and the more it was concealed the more suspicious we would look. If a guard found that manuscript, we hoped that he would simply confiscate it and let us go, reasoning that we were merely naïve about bringing such items into the country.

As the guard searched the back dash, he asked us what was in the package, picked it up, and tore off the wrapping. The manuscript lay exposed to full view, and the guard's hand even brushed across it. We could easily see the title of the manuscript from where we stood outside the car.

Apparently the guard never saw the manuscript. After searching for more than an hour, he waved us on.

A person may say the incident was happenstance, but we were keenly aware of the protecting, delivering power of God.

The next day we conducted a seminar for a group of about thirty ministers of an indigenous group that emerged from Pentecostal revivals in the 1920s. They believe strongly that the new birth consists of repentance, water baptism, and the baptism of the Holy Spirit, and they uphold standards of holiness in conduct and dress. Some of the ministers baptize in the name of Jesus but did not know its significance and had not received teaching on the oneness of God.

From 10:00 AM to 8:00 PM on Saturday and then in the Sunday service we taught the people as much Pentecostal doctrine as we could. We saw God work and people begin to comprehend and accept the message. Several received the Holy Spirit during the Sunday service. We sowed the seed and left the results to God.

In 1989 I was invited to return to Bulgaria. This time I went alone. In the third file pocket of my briefcase I carried another Bulgarian manuscript, entitled "The New Birth." The customs official asked to see only my briefcase. He pulled all the material out of the first pocket and checked it. He put his hand into the second pocket and checked it. And then, without checking the third pocket, he closed the briefcase! Was it a coincidence that he did not find the manuscript? Once again, I knew that God put His hand on the situation.

When we proclaim the gospel of Jesus Christ, God confirms His Word. We do not need to be intimidated by ideology, tradition, false religion, strange culture, intellectualism, humanism, materialism, or demonic opposition, for God has designed the gospel to be victorious in every situation.

Paul proclaimed, "I am not ashamed of the gospel of Christ: for it is the power of God unto salvation to every one that believeth" (Romans 1:16). Paul was eager to travel to Rome itself, the home of the richest, most powerful, most intellectual people of his world, for he knew that the gospel could penetrate even that worldly city (Romans 1:15). He boldly told King Agrippa, "I would to God that not only you, but also all who hear me today, might become both almost and altogether such as I am, except for these chains" (Acts 26:29, NKJV). He had greater spiritual power, peace, and joy than the king himself, and he was convinced that the gospel would work even for him.

Paul knew by experience that if he would simply preach "Jesus Christ, and him crucified," he would present the gospel "in demonstration of the Spirit and of power" (I Corinthians 2:2-4). God confirms the preaching of His Word and powerfully saves those who believe and obey the message.

Upon my arrival in Bulgaria the second time, I faced another problem. Some of the ministers had seemingly accepted our message, but some had not, and the expected open door was now shut. Plans were quickly changed. I rented a car and drove six hours to another part of the country where riots had erupted only a few weeks before. I ministered in a Pentecostal church, met with an influential trinitarian leader named Brother Daniel, and left my manuscript for the group to study. We discussed water baptism in the name of Jesus extensively, and I realized how difficult it would be for the leader to change his doctrinal position. Once again, I could only leave the results in the hands of God.

Shortly after my return to the United States, I received a letter from Sister Dora, a Bulgarian lady from our church in Austria who had initiated the contacts and translated the literature. She reported that as a result of the trip in 1988, several ministers and churches were now teaching Oneness and baptizing in the name of Jesus. Moreover, since the 1989 trip, Brother Daniel and several churches connected with him were baptizing in

Jesus' name. She related the following story:

"After a powerful message and prayer, during which a lady received the Holy Ghost and another lady received physical healing, we went down to the river to baptize some of the young men who had received the Holy Ghost. When Brother Daniel stepped into the water and baptized the first one in the name of Jesus [and] this fellow came out of this Jesus Name water, he began to cry, shout, [and] worship. [He] was shaken by such a power that Daniel could not hold him.

"[For] more than fifteen minutes he danced, jumped, and worshiped in the water, and the power of God fell upon the rest and we began to worship too. Some of the brothers told me that now they can see what a power is in the mighty name of Jesus. I believe that happened as a witness to all who had any doubts about Jesus Name baptism.

"After the brother calmed down, he [came] out of the water and told us that the moment he was baptized in Jesus' name, calling upon the name of Jesus, he saw a man clothed in white garments, light, and glory who pointed [out] to him a narrow path and said, 'Fear not, because from now on you will work for Me!'"

If we will preach the Word, God will confirm it!

On the same trip in 1989, I visited the Soviet Union with our missionaries to Finland, Brother and Sister Harold Kinney. In December 1988, Brother Balca had made the first direct contact with Oneness Pentecostals in the Soviet Union, the result of Andrew D. Urshan's revivals in Leningrad [now St. Petersburg] in 1915.

Shortly before our trip, the Kinneys made a preparatory visit to Leningrad. They learned that the Lord had spoken to the church in prophecy, saying that visitors from the West would soon come and help ignite a great revival that would sweep across the nation.

We prayed that the Lord would somehow use our visit to fulfill His plan. Our personal involvement was not important, but since we were among the first United Pentecostals to meet with and minister to this group, we felt that the outcome of our visit would be important for future efforts in the Soviet Union.

When we arrived in Leningrad in June 1989, we discovered that representatives of about fourteen churches in the Soviet Union had gathered to discuss the formation of a Oneness Pentecostal fellowship, now that they could exercise greater religious freedom. These representatives said that they were in contact with about 238 Oneness churches and had knowledge of about 27,000 believers.

Through extended dialogue, we confirmed that they believe strongly in the message of Oneness and in the new birth of baptism in Jesus' name and the baptism of the Holy Spirit. As they discussed among themselves issues of holiness and the doctrinal basis of the proposed organization, we explained the teachings of our international church and offered our help and fellowship. While we were trying to find out about their beliefs, they were trying to find out about ours. We prayed for the anointing of the Holy Spirit to confirm our message to their hearts and unite us in the Spirit and in the faith.

At the beginning of my message on Sunday morning I felt led to make a general statement: "I believe the Lord wants to fill someone with the Holy Spirit here today." At the time I did not realize how challenging this statement was or how the Lord would use it.

Over the years of persecution and isolation, the church

in Leningrad had developed the practice of praying in homes for people to receive the Holy Spirit. They did not have group prayer at the church, and the church services were usually restrained. As I preached, however, I saw people cry and shake as the Holy Spirit moved upon them.

At the conclusion of the service, the pastor's daughter began to pray with great anointing. When she finished, the pastor's son began to pray forcefully, shaking vehemently. An elder of the church became very upset at this demonstration. After the son became quiet, the service was dismissed. But God was not finished.

Later that afternoon we returned to the church sanctuary for a men's meeting. We spoke on doctrinal topics, including healing. At the close of the meeting, a preacher requested prayer for healing. Soon every man in the building came to the front for special prayer. As Brother Kinney and I laid hands upon them, they began to pray demonstratively, and the power of the Holy Spirit fell.

A young man came forward to testify: "I have just received the Holy Spirit!" Immediately the pastor said, "God has confirmed His Word. The preacher said that God wanted to fill someone with the Holy Spirit today, and He has. This noisy group prayer may disturb some, but it does not disturb God. It is somewhat unusual for us, but I do not think it is unusual for our guests. We need to learn how the church in the West conducts services."

At that, the elder who had been upset earlier began to speak forcefully. He testified, "I have not spoken in tongues in years, but today I have been renewed in the Holy Spirit!" Once again, God had confirmed His Word.

Three months later, the Kinneys visited Leningrad

again. They learned that over the summer the church had baptized sixty-one people in the name of Jesus—the beginning of what we pray and believe will be a mighty revival.

We do not know what will happen in the world in the days and months ahead. But we do not have to know. If we will boldly proclaim God's Word everywhere and to everyone, God will confirm it. He will reveal His truth to hungry hearts. He will fill with His Spirit those who repent and believe. He will anoint, protect, sustain, and deliver. He will support the preaching of the gospel with miracles, signs, and wonders. He will endow His witnesses with gifts of the Spirit for effective testimony and ministry. He will send His angels to protect and encourage, and He will bring victory over all satanic or demonic opposition.

This is how the gospel message was first proclaimed. It was "spoken by the Lord, and was confirmed unto us by them that heard him; God also bearing them witness, both with signs and wonders, and with divers miracles, and gifts of the Holy Ghost, according to his own will" (Hebrews 2:3-4). We should proclaim, pray for, and believe for the same move of the Holy Spirit today. As we do, we will surely see global revival.

Pentecostal Herald, April 1990

CHAPTER 25

Signs, Wonders, Miracles, and Gifts

How shall we escape if we neglect so great a salvation, which at the first began to be spoken by the Lord, and was confirmed to us by those who heard Him, God also bearing witness both with signs and wonders, with various miracles, and gifts of the Holy Spirit, according to His own will? (Hebrews 2:3-4, NKJV).

God answers prayer in our day. People been healed of serious medical conditions, to the amazement of doctors. Others have received jobs at a time of urgent need. Still others have been delivered from sin and filled with the Holy Spirit.

For the church to be spiritually healthy and to grow, we need the continual work of God's Spirit. We must always rely upon God's direction and power. We should expect signs, wonders, miracles, and gifts of the Spirit as God confirms His Word.

When Jesus gave the great commission, He promised that miraculous power would accompany all believers as they proclaimed the gospel. The early church carried out His instructions to preach everywhere, and the Lord confirmed the Word with signs following (Mark 16:15-20).

Just as Jesus promised, the preaching of the apostles was accompanied by casting out of demons, speaking in tongues, divine protection from accidental harm, and divine healing of the sick. These miracles were instrumental in attracting multitudes and adding believers to the church. (See Acts 2:6; 3:11; 5:12-14; 8:6-8, 13; 14:3.)

Paul stated that his missionary ministry was accomplished "in mighty signs and wonders, by the power of the Spirit of God, so that from Jerusalem and round about to Illyricum I have fully preached the gospel of Christ" (Romans 15:19, NKJV). The key to his ministerial success was not "persuasive words of human wisdom, but in demonstration of the Spirit and of power" (I Corinthians 2:4, NKJV).

Paul listed nine supernatural gifts of the Spirit that assist in building up the church. "But the manifestation of the Spirit is given to each one for the profit of all": the word of wisdom, the word of knowledge, faith, gifts of healings, the working of miracles, prophecy, discerning of spirits, different kinds of tongues, and the interpretation of tongues (I Corinthians 12:7-10, NKJV). It is God's will for these gifts to be manifested in every local body of believers until the second coming of Christ. (See I Corinthians 1:2, 7.) His Word admonishes us, "Pursue love, and desire spiritual gifts" (I Corinthians 14:1, NKJV).

"We do not wrestle against flesh and blood, but against principalities, against powers, against the rulers of the darkness of this age, against spiritual hosts of wickedness in the heavenly places" (Ephesians 6:12,

NKJV). Therefore, we need spiritual weapons, not merely human programs and methods. To be victorious, we must have the miraculous work of the Holy Spirit.

Let's seek God for signs, wonders, miracles, and gifts of the Spirit—not for our glory but to advance the kingdom of God. Let's believe that God can use each one of us as an instrument of His grace and power to reach others with the gospel.

New Life News, Austin, Texas, Fall 2004. Scripture quotations are from the NKJV.

CHAPTER 26

Supernatural Spiritual Gifts

Supernatural spiritual gifts are indispensable in the life of a healthy church. They strengthen believers and confirm the gospel to unbelievers. Sometimes they make the difference between victory and defeat.

In the fall of 1995, our three-year-old church in Austin, Texas, faced an urgent need. We had completely filled our rented building and needed to build our own facility if we wanted to grow. Over a two-year period, we had purchased property, developed architectural plans, obtained site and building permits, and secured financing. When we got ready to build, however, we found that we needed an extra $100,000 because of special requirements and the construction boom at that time. The situation seemed hopeless.

One Thursday, we had a prayer meeting at church. At the close, a young man burst forth with tongues and interpretation. The Lord told us: "You can't see healing, but I see healing. You can't see a miracle, but I see a miracle. You can't see a new building, but I see a new building."

Instantly we felt a strong witness of the Spirit. My mother-in-law was healed that night of a back injury.

During the next midweek service, my wife's grandfather was brought back to life in the midst of a stroke. By that Friday, a major bank in Austin approved us for a building loan at the full amount we needed, with a lower interest rate that left our mortgage payment about the same as previously budgeted. Thus, a week after the initial word from the Lord, we saw a healing, a miracle, and approval for our new building.

The apostolic church was characterized by signs and wonders that attracted people to the gospel and enabled the church to growth (Acts 2:43; 4:33). I Corinthians 12 speaks of nine spiritual "gifts"—miraculous endowments that operate by the power of the Holy Spirit. Let us look briefly at the nature of these gifts.

The originator is the Holy Spirit. (See I Corinthians 12:4-11.) While the gifts differ, the one true God is the author of them all. He is the one who performs the work by His Spirit.

The gifts are supernatural. This passage describes them as "works" of God and as the "manifestation of the Spirit." It is a mistake to define them in terms of natural human abilities.

They are given according to God's will. There is great value in learning about spiritual gifts and learning to yield to God's Spirit so that we are prepared for God to use us. But no human can grant such a gift to someone or exercise such a gift at will. God is the one who bestows and enables the gifts according to His sovereign purpose. (See I Corinthians 12:11; Hebrews 2:4.)

We must exercise gifts according to God's Word. We must regulate ourselves lest we misuse the gifts. (See I Corinthians 14:32.)

Specifically, we must operate all gifts with love for God and each other, not out of pride, strife, manipulation, or attempt to control others. Without love, they are worthless. (See I Corinthians 13:1-8.)

They are to glorify God. We should always draw attention to what God, not a human, is doing. It is troubling when the primary emphasis is on a human personality or the exercise of a particular gift in itself. For instance, gifts of healing are often effective in building faith and sparking a revival that leads many people to salvation. (See Acts 3:1-11; 4:4.) But if a meeting or a ministry focuses on healing while neglecting the message of salvation, then God's purpose in granting healing is not fully accomplished.

They are given for times of special need. In the church, the supernatural gifts should be normal, not abnormal; expected, not unexpected. They do not operate continually, however. If they did, we would not think of them as supernatural. To illustrate, in the Gospels and Acts multitudes were healed and a number of people were raised from the dead. Nevertheless, all the members of the early church eventually died without being raised again, and presumably most died of some illness or disease that was not healed.

There is diversity of gifts, but their purpose is to build up the entire body (I Corinthians 12:4-6, 12-26). Different people exercise different gifts, but all should do so for the good of the body. We must value the unique contributions that each person can make to the whole.

Every local church should seek spiritual gifts through prayer and Bible study. As we do, we will see the manifestations of the Spirit in our midst. Our churches will grow, and lives will be transformed by the power of the gospel.

South Texas Vision, September-October 2004

CHAPTER 27

Growing with the Increase of God

"Let my people grow!" Thus cries out the title of a book on church growth by Tim Massengale, putting a spin on the words Moses spoke to Pharaoh. Growth is characteristic of every living organism, and growth must be a high priority for the church of the living God.

But what kind of growth are we talking about? Colossians 2:19 tells us how the right kind of growth comes: The church, which is the body of Christ, "holds[s] fast to the Head, from whom all the body, nourished and knit together by joints and ligaments, grows with the increase that is from God" (NKJV). True church growth, which encompasses both numerical growth and growth in spiritual maturity, will only come as the church remains closely connected to Jesus Christ. As it does, it will grow with the increase that comes from God, not an increase that comes merely from human ability and ingenuity.

The church of the first century grew phenomenally as it remained connected to the Lord in four areas: (1) doctrinal truth, (2) unity and fellowship among believers, (3) prayer, and (4) worship. "And they continued stedfastly in

181

the apostles' doctrine and fellowship, and in breaking of bread, and in prayers. . . . And they, continuing daily with one accord in the temple, and breaking bread from house to house, did eat their meat with gladness and singleness of heart, praising God, and having favour with all the people. And the Lord added to the church daily such as should be saved" (Acts 2:42, 46-47).

In our day it is exciting to be part of an international fellowship of apostolic believers who adhere to these same goals. The United Pentecostal Church International staunchly affirms the message and experience of the apostolic church of Acts 2.

The word "United" in our name reminds us that the organization was founded with the desire of uniting all brethren of like precious faith under one banner for the cause of proclaiming "the whole gospel to the whole world" and establishing a worldwide fellowship of believers.

The word "Pentecostal" in our name refers to our determination to emulate the pattern established in Acts 2 on the Day of Pentecost. Our Fundamental Doctrine advocates the salvation message of Acts 2:38—repentance, water baptism in the name of Jesus Christ, and the baptism of the Holy Spirit. Our commitment to holiness of life is likewise a vital aspect of adherence to the apostles' doctrine, for as the apostle Peter exhorted in Acts 2:40, we must save ourselves from our perverse generation.

The word "Church" reminds us that we are not just an organization of individuals, whether ministers or saints, but an integral, vital part of the body of Christ that exists to worship, pray, and proclaim the gospel. Our World Network of Prayer helps to harness our energies for prayer, and our numerous camp meetings and conferences continually ignite and renew our worship.

The word "International" confirms that we have formed a worldwide fellowship to which the Lord is adding daily. We now have constituents in about 135 nations around the globe [179 as of 2006].

Because of our commitment to these apostolic priorities, God has indeed blessed us with the growth that comes from Him. From about 500 churches in 1945, we have grown to almost 4,000 in the United States and Canada and 20,000 in the rest of the world in 1997. Our worldwide constituency is approaching 3,000,000. These numbers reflect respectable growth over the last half century in North America and spectacular growth in many countries in the last decade.

Of course, we understand that neither the name nor the organization is necessary or sufficient for salvation. Salvation is by grace through faith, purchased by the atoning sacrifice of Jesus Christ, and experienced by all who obey the gospel of Jesus Christ. It is not our place to judge other groups or individuals, nor can we claim to be the only group who embraces truth and has an experience with God. But we should be thankful to belong to a fellowship that has a leading role in evangelizing the world with the whole gospel, preserving the fullness of the apostolic message, and contending earnestly for the faith once delivered to the saints. (See Jude 3.)

In the early part of the twentieth century, most Pentecostals in various organizations—trinitarian as well as Oneness—had a strong commitment to the areas we have identified, including the Pentecostal message of the baptism of the Holy Spirit, holiness of life, fervency of prayer, and heartfelt worship. Indeed, the guiding impulse of all these organizations was the restoration of apostolic Christianity.

Unfortunately, the trinitarian Pentecostals chose to follow historical tradition, creedal orthodoxy, and majority opinion instead of returning fully to the apostolic pattern and biblical teaching of the oneness of God, absolute deity of Jesus Christ, and water baptism in the name of Jesus Christ. Their decision proved to be a harbinger of things to come, for many trinitarian Pentecostals are now in the process of discarding or deemphasizing many truths they once held dear.

For instance, the key distinctive of the entire Pentecostal movement from the outset has been the baptism of the Holy Spirit with the initial sign of speaking in tongues. Many trinitarian Pentecostals and most charismatics, however, now deny that speaking in tongues is the initial evidence. In classical trinitarian Pentecostal churches, usually only a minority of members now claim the baptism of the Holy Spirit. Some scholars' estimate for the Assemblies of God is as low as thirty percent.

Likewise, all Pentecostals once held very similar standards of holiness in conduct and dress, but gradually one organization after another has abandoned them. In recent years, observers have also noticed a decline in the fervor of prayer and worship among trinitarian Pentecostals. Indeed, prominent trinitarian scholars have acknowledged that if people want to see the type of demonstrative worship that characterized all Pentecostals until quite recently, they should attend a United Pentecostal camp meeting or conference.

Through the years, trinitarian Pentecostals have generally tried to ignore the existence of Oneness Pentecostals, apparently in hopes that their influence would be minimal and that they would dwindle away. But today apostolic believers are more visible and active than ever.

In what appears to be a major change of direction, *Charisma* magazine, the leading periodical of the charismatic movement, devoted a feature article to Oneness Pentecostals, particularly United Pentecostals. It noted their significant impact in such areas as gospel music and witness to high governmental officials, including the president of the United States. It seems that trinitarian Pentecostals and charismatics are finally acknowledging that we Oneness Pentecostals are here to stay and that it is important to hear what we have to say.

As one might expect, *Charisma* criticized Oneness Pentecostals for our emphasis on doctrinal teaching and practical holiness of life. After all, over the years the charismatic movement has strongly opposed both emphases and has been a major factor in causing the classical trinitarian Pentecostals to abandon them. (It has also had a positive influence upon many people, especially those with no Pentecostal background, by encouraging them to seek after the things of God.) *Charisma* acknowledged that the doctrine of the trinity is a mystery, that the apostles baptized in Jesus' name, and that United Pentecostals hold to the standards of holiness that all Pentecostals once embraced as scriptural. Yet it argued that our stand for the oneness of God, baptism in Jesus' name, and practical holiness are not important in the modern world.

Somewhat wistfully, the article offered the hope (from charismatics' point of view) that the United Pentecostal Church might change its fundamental position on these points, although it did not offer any solid supporting evidence. Why should charismatics have such a strong desire to see us change? It may be that as long as we hold firm to these apostolic truths, our very existence reproves their unwillingness to stand for them. Moreover, as long as we continue to grow while adhering to these positions, we disprove the notion that the church can no longer survive or increase in the modern world if it insists on maintaining its apostolic identity.

Among many Pentecostals and charismatics, the motivating factor for abandoning basic doctrine and holiness is not a profound change of theological views after intense prayer and Bible study, but simply a desire to grow at all costs—to achieve greater acceptance and "success." Some such churches have mushroomed by affirming or ignoring lifestyle choices that are clearly contrary to God's Word; by emphasizing showmanship, entertainment, recreation, and social life; and by openly appealing to members of other churches even though they consider them to be already saved.

But such growth should not impress us, for it is not the increase that comes from God. It is possible to amass a crowd of thousands in a year's time with relatively little spiritual effort, but true growth requires a new birth, conversion from sin, a change of lifestyle, attainment of maturity, and a disciplined life. This kind of growth takes time, effort, intensive prayer, one-on-one ministry, and the miraculous work of the Holy Spirit.

We should not be surprised if many people, even professing Christians, follow the route of doctrinal compromise and worldly lifestyle. Paul predicted, "For the time will come when they will not endure sound doctrine; but after their own lusts shall they heap to themselves teachers, having itching ears; and they shall turn away their ears from the truth, and shall be turned unto fables" (II Timothy 4:3-4). Jesus Himself said, "Enter ye in at the strait gate: for wide is the gate, and broad is the way, that leadeth to destruction, and many there be which go in thereat: because strait is the gate, and narrow is the way, which leadeth unto life, and few there be that find it" (Matthew 7:13-14).

Do these prophetic utterances mean that we should not expect significant church growth? Absolutely not! As in the Book of Acts, it is God's will for us to have revival and increase until Jesus comes! These passages simply remind us that we must not sacrifice our apostolic identity—including our fundamental doctrine, our lifestyle of holiness, and our fervency of prayer and worship—in a mistaken attempt to attain any kind of growth at any kind of cost.

No, it is our message and identity that have enabled us to grow so rapidly without compromise, have forced others to take notice of us, that speak to their conscience so strongly that they are determined to change us. Let us continue to proclaim the whole gospel to the whole world, and in doing so we will grow with the increase that comes from God. As we continue in the apostles' doctrine and fellowship, in prayer and in praise, the Lord will add to the church daily those who should be saved.

Pentecostal Herald, September 1997

CHAPTER 28

A Faithful Servant

Serving the Lord is our greatest responsibility and also our greatest privilege. As Apostolics we treasure the beautiful truths of the Bible, especially the doctrines of the Incarnation, the Atonement, the oneness of God, the deity of Jesus, salvation by grace through faith, repentance, water baptism in the name of Jesus Christ, the baptism of the Holy Spirit, holiness of life, the gifts of the Spirit, and liberty in worship. We must never forsake this New Testament heritage.

At the same time, we can never reduce Christianity to a set of beliefs or practices. It must involve our entire life and our entire being. We can summarize it in the words of Jesus: "Follow me." This command is so simple that a child can obey it, yet it is so profound that we spend a lifetime seeking to fulfill it. We experience New Testament salvation by believing and obeying the gospel of Jesus Christ; we experience New Testament life and ministry by serving our Lord and Savior Jesus Christ.

"And [Jesus] said to them all, If any man will come after me, let him deny himself, and take up his cross daily, and follow me. For whosoever will save his life shall lose it: but whosoever will lose his life for my sake, the same shall save it. For what is a man advantaged, if he gain the whole world, and lose himself, or be cast away?" (Luke 9:23-25).

Each of us has different talents, abilities, and gifts, yet all are called to follow the Lord and serve Him. Not all of us can achieve great success as humans count success—whether in secular life or even in church life. But all of us can be faithful to our gifts and calling, and that is the true measure of success in God's kingdom. "Moreover it is required in stewards, that a man be found faithful" (I Corinthians 4:2).

Ministers and leaders must have a servant's heart—serving God and serving the people of God. "But Jesus called [the disciples] unto him, and said, Ye know that the princes of the Gentiles exercise dominion over them, and they that are great exercise authority upon them. But it shall not be so among you: but whosoever will be great among you, let him be your minister; and whosoever will be chief among you, let him be your servant: even as the Son of man came not to be ministered unto, but to minister, and to give his life a ransom for many" (Matthew 20:25-28).

The apostle Peter admonished: "The elders who are among you I exhort, I who am a fellow elder and a witness of the sufferings of Christ, and also a partaker of the glory that will be revealed: Shepherd the flock of God which is among you, serving as overseers, not by compulsion but willingly, not for dishonest gain but eagerly; nor as being lords over those entrusted to you, but being examples to the flock; and when the Chief Shepherd appears, you will receive the crown of glory that does not fade away" (I Peter 5:1-4, NKJV).

Ultimately, the goal for which we should strive is not to preach the best sermon, sing the best song, or pastor the best church, but to hear these words of our Lord, as He wipes away the tears of every trial: "Well done, good and faithful servant; thou hast been faithful over a few things, I will make thee ruler over many things: enter thou into the joy of thy [Lord]" (Matthew 25:23).

South Texas Vision, July-August 2006

CHAPTER 29

Favoritism and the Church

Modern society expresses great concern for the evils caused by various forms of favoritism. For example, in the United States it is illegal to discriminate on the basis of race or gender in education, housing, and business. The civil service system is designed to eliminate the hiring of unqualified people on the basis of family ties or friendship. In fact, no federal official, not even the president, can hire a close relative. Most publicly held corporations have similar rules designed to prevent nepotism and cronyism.

Biblical Teaching

The Bible strongly opposes all forms of favoritism, especially in the church. James 2:1-3 denounces those who show partiality because of social or economic status. James 2:9 bluntly says that favoritism is sinful: "But if you show partiality, you commit sin" (NKJV). James 3:17 contrasts favoritism and hypocrisy with divine wisdom. God shows no partiality (Acts 10:34; Romans 2:11; Galatians 2:6), and He forbids His people to do so (Job

13:10). Leaders are to judge all matters fairly, regardless of who is involved (Leviticus 19:15; Deuteronomy 1:17; 16:19).

In Christ, there is no unequal treatment based on race, social class, or gender (Galatians 3:28). In other words, Christ's body—the church—must be free of discrimination. Paul solemnly admonished Timothy to perform his pastoral duties without favoritism: "I charge thee before God, and the Lord Jesus Christ, and the elect angels, that thou observe these things without preferring one before another, doing nothing by partiality" (I Timothy 5:21). This instruction has particular relevance to ordaining people prematurely or giving them a position for which they are not qualified, for the very next verse says, "Lay hands suddenly on no man, neither be partaker of other men's sins: keep thyself pure" (I Timothy 5:22).

How should the church implement the scriptural teaching against favoritism?

Prejudice

First, the church must stand unequivocally against all forms of prejudice. Every local church must actively welcome any human being, for the great commission is the responsibility of every believer and every body of believers. A person of any color, race, or national origin should be able to visit, attend, and become a member of any of our churches without experiencing either overt harassment and intimidation or subtle social pressure and ostracism.

As a matter of evangelistic strategy, it is necessary to establish churches that minister to people of minority language groups, to plant churches in minority neighborhoods, and to help preachers who are members of minority groups to start churches. This does not mean, however, that we are to think in terms of "white" churches and "black" churches. Each church should simply be a local extension of *the* church, the body of Christ, and as such it must be open to everyone and have fellowship on an equal basis with all other churches.

As a matter of personal holiness, we must train our people, beginning with the children, to abhor prejudice. Those who hate their brothers and sisters are murderers in God's sight and do not have eternal life (I John 3:15). If this statement is true of those who hate an individual who has wronged them, how much more it is true of those who hate an entire class of people without cause? Christians are to love all people, even their enemies, and especially their fellow believers (Matthew 5:43-44; John 13:34-35). Racist groups such as the Ku Klux Klan are incompatible with Christianity, and prejudice will destroy holiness in a Christian's life.

God's church must not condone or promote racial segregation. Some may argue that we must not offend unbelievers who are prejudiced, but this argument often seems to promote the prejudices of believers. Moreover, should the church merely conform to the sinful attitudes of society? At what point should it confront society's false values and seek to transform society? If we refuse to discard other holiness teachings in order to be more acceptable to worldly society, why should we condone the sin of prejudice? If we plan to be among the saints from every race and tongue who will worship God together in eternity, why should we object to worshiping with our brothers and sisters on earth?

195

Jesus commanded us to preach the gospel to "every creature" (Mark 16:15) and to make disciples of "all nations" (Matthew 28:19). In the latter verse, the Greek word for "nation" is *ethnos*, which literally means "race or ethnic group." The church needs to consider seriously how it can fulfill the biblical mandate to reach out to all ethnic groups in every locality. If a local church refuses to minister to people of a certain race or class in its immediate area, then it is not evangelizing its community. The church should also consider how it can include minority groups in all facets of corporate church life. At all levels, opportunities for fellowship, ministry, and leadership should be open to everyone equally—in practice as well as in theory.

Elitism

The world also threatens the church with a more subtle form of favoritism: elitism, or control by an elite group. Many factors—wealth, talent, social ties, family ties, tradition—tend to create an aristocracy, or privileged class, in human institutions, and the church is not immune to such influences. New converts can feel locked out of a system that gives preference to old, established families. Young ministers can become frustrated with the lack of opportunities available to those who do not have an influential minister to promote them.

How can the church minimize such elitist pressures? *First*, those who have attained prominence or "success" should take care to lead lives of modesty and moderation. They must not become competitive or extravagant with such things as clothes, houses, automobiles, other material possessions, and even church buildings. They should not indulge in a lifestyle far above the average church member or the average preacher, even if they or their church can afford it.

Second, each person must constantly fight against exclusiveness, cliquishness, and snobbishness in his or her own life, refusing to allow social classes to develop in the church. Preachers should avoid cultivating only an inner circle of select friends. They must not evaluate their own or others' success by the wealth or social status of the people in their churches. They should be willing to preach for any church, regardless of its size, composition, or financial ability. They should be genuinely friendly toward everyone, even toward those with no "name" and no ability to help them.

Third, the greatest emphasis and recognition should not be given to talent or to outward standards of success, but to faithfulness. For example, it is convenient to promote someone with great musical or oratorical ability despite their failures in areas of holiness or spirituality. It is likewise easy to cater to a person who has wealth, education, high social standing, family ties, or great influence in the church. However, such a practice will create an elite group of people who receive special favors and are granted special exceptions, and it will result in carnality, hypocrisy, and disillusionment.

Nepotism and Cronyism

Most human beings have special love for family members and close friends. This love is natural and commendable; yet when it causes favoritism in the church, God's Word is violated. God removed Eli's family from the priesthood because Eli allowed his sons to exercise that

197

office despite their sins and lack of spiritual qualifications.

Ministers must guard against giving special prefer-ences, unfair advantages, or special exceptions to family members and personal friends. The New Testament min-istry is not a lineal priesthood, nor is the local church a family business or a hereditary kingdom. Moreover, God's will is not accomplished by personal manipulation or political maneuvering. Pastors are not the owners of a private company with absolute discretionary power, but they are stewards of God's business. As such, they are accountable to God and to the people of God. The princi-ples of God's Word must guide their decisions and override their personal feelings.

Under what circumstances is it appropriate for a minister to appoint family members and personal friends to positions in the church or to use them in prominent capacities? For example, when is it proper for a pastor to place a son on the church ministerial staff or recom-mend that he become the pastor's successor? The Bible provides guidelines that should apply to everyone equally, whether or not the person has personal ties to the pastor.

First, pastors must genuinely know that the choice is the will of God. They should not automatically presume that it is, just because it seems pleasing to them, nor should they merely ask God to ratify their own predeter-mined plan. Rather, they should honestly and diligently seek direction from the Holy Spirit. If it is the will of God, there will be no need to manipulate or to force others to acquiesce.

Second, the person must be spiritually qualified for the position or role. For example, the Bible lists explicit qualifications for deacons and elders (pastors). The person's qualifications should be examined sympathetically but as objectively as possible.

Third, pastors must give other people the same or equal opportunities. They have a responsibility to train and develop all whom God has entrusted in their care. For example, if pastors promote the ministry of their own children, they should give other young ministers in their church equal opportunities to be used there or give them equal assistance in getting started elsewhere.

Often, family members will be more qualified in certain roles because of their experience and training, but pastors still have the responsibility to qualify others and to provide opportunities for others to develop their potential. For example, even if family members are the most capable musically, other church people need to be used and trained as well.

Fourth, the person chosen for a leadership role must have the goodwill, respect, and approval of the people. And respect cannot be demanded; it must be earned. People may be appointed to a position of ministry, but unless they have influence with the body of believers they will not actually exercise an effective ministry among them.

The apostles did not arbitrarily choose deacons to handle church business; rather, they asked the congregation to choose seven spiritually qualified men whom they could appoint (Acts 6:2-6). Paul and Barnabas were called by the Holy Spirit, but their calling was recognized by the church (Acts 13:1-3). Our form of church government provides that the congregation elect the pastor, and it is unethical to subvert this process.

As a practical matter, it is advisable for young preachers to establish their own ministry in another place without relying heavily upon someone else's reputation and influence. In this way they will develop self-confidence and confidence in their own calling. On their own, they will learn how to trust God and how to follow the Spirit. The people back in their home churches will learn to respect them and to view them as ministers in their own right.

Finally, those who are used in a certain capacity must perform their task faithfully and well. The pastor should help them overcome faults, problems, and inconsistencies. It is imperative that the pastor not overlook sin or false doctrine but uphold scriptural standards of holiness and discipline. Pastors must apply these standards equally to everyone. It can be extremely painful to do so when family is involved, but this is the risk pastors take and the responsibility they accept when they appoint a family member to a position.

Nepotism and cronyism are not just local church concerns. The church as a whole must actively cultivate opportunities for young ministers who do not have family connections or who are converts to Pentecost. The church needs the constant influx of new blood and new ideas into the ministry. Established preachers should make a special effort to befriend young ministers who need help in getting started.

God does not play favorites; therefore, we cannot blame the will of God if certain categories of people seem to be favored disproportionately in the church. The church is not perfect and never will be until the Lord's coming, but we can and should work to make it as free from favoritism, prejudice, and bias as possible. The Holy Spirit, who pours out divine love in our hearts, will help us to accomplish this task if we will be sensitive to Him.

Forward, April-June 1988

CHAPTER 30

God's Minimum Requirements for Preachers

Only God can call a person to the preaching ministry, but God's church must recognize and approve that ministry (Acts 13:2-4; I Timothy 4:14). Jesus commended the Ephesian church for testing those who claimed to be apostles but were not (Revelation 2:2).

Preachers are ordained by the church, and in order for the church to do so, those seeking ordination must meet certain qualifications (Titus 1:5). God's initial call does not automatically qualify people; they must qualify themselves according to God's Word, and the church must evaluate and approve their qualifications.

Moreover, it is possible for ministers to lose their scriptural qualifications, in which case the church has the authority and responsibility to relieve them of their leadership position. The early church wrote letters of commendation for those who were approved as ministers among them, but the apostles also wrote warnings for churches not to receive certain ministers who had fallen into false doctrine or sin. Hymenaeus, Alexander, and Philetus were once in the faith but became false teachers and were removed from fellowship by Paul (I Timothy 1:19-20; II Timothy 2:17-18). John warned the church not to receive Diotrephes, a minister who had fallen into the sins of pride, rebellion, slander, and division (III John 9-10). Demas lost his ministry because of his love for the world (II Timothy 4:10).

Some argue that because no one can touch God's anointed, the church does not have any right to examine the ministry. While rebellion against God's leader is wrong, God has placed authority over leaders themselves, so that they too are subject to discipline. Even the highest leaders must submit to one another and to the collective body. Peter, the recognized apostle to the Jews, and Paul, the apostle to the Gentiles, acknowledged the authority of the council in Jerusalem to question their activities and to pronounce decisions binding upon everyone. It is also interesting that Paul rebuked Peter when the latter deviated from Christian principles (Galatians 2:11-14).

Just as the church has authority to examine and approve ministerial candidates, so it has authority to remove people from a ministerial position if they no longer meet God's requirements. Actually they disqualify themselves by their actions, and the church simply recognizes this fact. Solomon permanently removed Abiathar from the high priesthood, a hereditary role explicitly ordained by God, because of his rebellion (I Kings 2:26-27).

The Pastoral Epistles—I and II Timothy and Titus—are filled with admonitions and instructions for preachers. Particularly, I Timothy 3:1-7 and Titus 1:5-9 list twenty-three minimum requirements for anyone who aspires to be a preacher or pastor. These passages use the words *elder* and *bishop* (literally, "overseer") inter-changeably to refer to a leader, overseer, or shepherd of a local church. (See Acts 20:17, 28; I Peter 5:1-4.) This office includes those who rule (lead) the church and those who preach and teach the Word (I Timothy 5:17). The requirements are listed below, with definitions and explanations based on the Greek text.

Requirements Listed in Both Passages

1. *Blameless*: above reproach, unreprovable. Titus states this twice and explains the reason why it is impor-tant: the overseer is the steward of God's work. If ministers are not blameless, they bring reproach upon the church and upon God. They will cause unbelievers to blaspheme the name of God because of their evil deeds (Romans 2:24).

2. *Husband of one wife*: not a polygamist. Since no Christians were allowed to live in polygamy, many com-mentators say this excludes former polygamists or those who divorce and remarry without scriptural authority. We should note that the purpose of this phrase is not to exclude women from ministry, but it states a general prin-ciple in masculine terms. If read so woodenly as to exclude women from ministry, it would also exclude single men, contrary to the examples of John the Baptist, Jesus, and Paul. In essence, it means "a person of strict morality."

3. *Sober*: sensible, of sound mind, prudent, self-con-trolled.

4. *Given to (lover of) hospitality*: hospitable; liter-ally, "stranger-loving."

5. *Not given to wine*: not a winebibber, not drunken.

6. *No striker*: not violent.

7. *Not greedy of filthy lucre*: not greedy for base gain, not pursuing dishonest gain.

8. *One that ruleth well his own house, having his children in subjection with all gravity*: controlling their own household with dignity and respect. If pastors cannot lead their own families, they will be unable to take care of the house of God. Titus states that the elder must have "faithful [believing] children not accused of riot [profligacy] or unruly [insubordination]"; that is, "a man whose children believe and are not open to the charge of being wild and disobedient" (NIV).

In other words, ministers must have a Christian household. The children will not be perfect, but they must have respect for the minister and the minister's teachings. Ministers cannot force their children to live for God, especially older teenagers and young adults. Nevertheless, as long as the children live in the home, the minister can require them to obey godly principles there and can refuse to support them financially in sinful activities.

Additional Requirements in I Timothy

9. *Vigilant*: temperate, clear-headed.

10. *Of good behavior*: well-behaved, orderly.

11. *Apt to teach*: competent (able) to teach.

12. *Patient*: gentle, forbearing.

13. *Not a brawler*: not contentious, not quarrelsome.

14. *Not covetous*: not greedy, not a lover of money

15. *Not a novice*: not a recent convert, not without experience. It is important not to elevate such a one too quickly because he or she may easily fall by pride, as the devil did.

16. *Have a good report of them which are without*: having a good reputation with outsiders. This is especially important so that the minister will not fall into reproach (disgrace) and into the snare (trap) of the devil.

Additional Requirements in Titus

17. *Not selfwilled*: not self-pleasing, not overbearing.

18. *Not soon angry*: not quick-tempered.

19. *Lover of good men*: one who loves what is good (people or things).

20. *Just*: upright, right in conduct.

21. *Holy*: separated from sin and the world and dedicated to God and His will.

22. *Temperate*: self-controlled, disciplined.

23. *Holding fast the faithful word*: doctrinally sound, and thereby able both to exhort believers and to convict those who contradict truth. "He must hold firmly to the trustworthy message as it has been taught, so that he can encourage others by sound doctrine and refute those who oppose it" (NIV).

Character and Reputation

God emphasizes the character and reputation of preachers: preachers must be blameless (stated three times) and have a good report in the community. This means more than membership or good standing in the church. It means more than forgiveness, which all Christians have received and can obtain again if they sin. If a ministerial candidate once lived a notorious life of sin, meeting these qualifications may take considerable time.

Why is it so important to meet them? If leaders have a blemished reputation in or out of the church, people will lack confidence in their leadership, counsel, and example. They will bring disgrace upon the church. Moreover, if they have certain character flaws or weaknesses, the pressures of leadership may be too much for them. The pastoral role may subject them to certain temptations that they do not handle well, and Satan may use this fact to trap them.

Preachers may fall into major sin, be forgiven by God, be restored to the church, and even be restored to many areas of service, but this does not automatically entitle them to their former position of leadership. They must once again meet the qualifications of being blameless, having a good report, and so on. This takes much time, and in some cases total restoration may never be possible. As an analogy, God can forgive church treasurers who embezzle, but it may never be wise for them to fill that office again, for their sake or for others' sake. The same is true of a Boy Scout leader who falls into homosexuality or a youth teacher who divorces his wife and marries one of his students. Moreover, some sins— such as child molestation, incest, and rape—may indicate deep personality problems that would permanently disqualify someone from many leadership positions.

Some may wonder why certain sins are not explicitly mentioned as disqualifications. The answer is that they are obviously covered in the rest of Scripture and are covered implicitly by the broader categories listed. For example, murder is not named, but it is encompassed by "no striker, not a brawler, blameless, good report, of good behavior, not soon angry, just, holy." Because of the seriousness of this offense in Scripture and in society (Genesis 9:5-6), it is unlikely that a pastor who commits murder could ever be restored to this office. Although David continued as king despite his murder of Uriah, his office was that of an Old Testament political ruler, not a priest, prophet, or New Testament preacher. Moreover, he, his family, and his nation continued to suffer because of that sin.

Sexual Sins

It appears that one of the greatest temptations facing the ministry is sex. How does sexual purity relate to God's requirements? Sexual immorality is clearly excluded by the requirements of "blameless, good report, good behavior, just, holy, and husband of one wife." Again, a sexual sin is an obvious disqualification in light of all the Scriptures. "But whoso committeth adultery with a woman lacketh understanding: he that doeth it destroyeth his own soul. A wound and dishonour shall he get; and his reproach shall not be wiped away" (Proverbs 6:32-33). Even our sinful society acknowledges the truth in this verse to some degree, as exemplified by the public reaction to scandals involving religious leaders. Even people guilty of sexual sins often expect their leaders to uphold moral standards publicly, particularly religious leaders who claim to be morally pure.

According to I Corinthians 6:15-18, sexual sins are unique in that only they are sins against one's own body. God has ordained that husband and wife become one flesh. Marriage is a holy institution and a type of Christ and the church. Sexual infidelity is a violation of the most basic, sacred, and intimate covenant that two people can make. Far from being a temporary lapse or indiscretion, it signals a fundamental breakdown of spirituality, character, and integrity—in relation to God, one's closest loved ones, and oneself. The offender has broken faith and trust in the most important stewardship he or she has. This is doubly true when this sin has been committed repeatedly, as it often is, or when it has been committed with someone who is under the care of the leader.

The Temptation of Money

God also places great emphasis on correct attitudes towards money, another great temptation facing the ministry. Not only must preachers reject all schemes for illegal, immoral, or unethical profit, they must not be covetous at all. Greed must not be a motivating factor in their lives.

Preachers should seriously question their spiritual well-being if their decisions are influenced significantly by monetary concerns, or if their standard of living rises significantly above that of the members of their church, their community, or their peers. They must be temperate and sober in all areas; this includes moderation and modesty in housing, transportation, clothing, recreation, vacations, and material possessions.

We can learn many additional lessons from the list of God's requirements for preachers. The aspiring candidates and those who ordain them need to consider each biblical qualification carefully. Every preacher of the gospel should continually measure his or her life by God's requirements in order to maintain His high, holy standard for the ministry.

Forward, January-March 1988

CHAPTER 31

The Paradox of Preaching

For after that in the wisdom of God the world by wisdom knew not God, it pleased God by the foolishness of preaching to save them that believe (I Corinthians 1:21).

What is the most effective way to salvage a marriage that is breaking up? To help an alcoholic escape his or her addiction? To reform a criminal? To heal a broken heart? To help people overcome the effects of child or spousal abuse? To encourage the depressed? To bring hope to those suffering from physical or emotional illness?

Doctors, lawyers, social workers, and secular counselors try hard to answer these questions. Their work is commendable, but their progress is often slow, limited, or temporary. At best, they provide assistance for this life but not for the life to come.

The church offers an answer that seems foolish in the eyes of the world, but paradoxically it is the single most effective means of life transformation. That answer is the preaching of the gospel. It is almost absurd to think that by one person's speaking exuberantly for about thirty minutes many people's lives can be changed forever, but that is exactly what happens in Pentecostal churches every Sunday. One anointed message can be the turning point for someone's life. Over time, messages from the Word of God become building blocks in the believer's spiritual life, stepping-stones in the believer's pathway to heaven.

On the Day of Pentecost, the apostle Peter stood and addressed thousands of people. A few weeks earlier, many of them had boisterously demanded the crucifixion of Jesus. When Peter bluntly declared that by their wicked hands they had slain the Lord, there was every reason to expect that they would call for his own crucifixion. Instead they were convicted of their sins and cried out, "Men and brethren, what shall we do?" (Acts 2:37). Anointed preaching made the difference. It brought them to a place of faith and repentance, so that three thousand were baptized in Jesus' name and filled with the Holy Spirit.

In New Testament times, preaching about the cross was seemingly an obstacle to evangelism. To the Jews, it was offensive to think that their Messiah—whom they thought would bring political deliverance and military victory—was actually killed by the Roman oppressors. The preaching of the cross was a stumbling block. To the Gentiles, there was tolerance for and even interest in a variety of religious and philosophical ideas, but the message that salvation comes through a man who died, and that this man had risen from the dead by an impossible miracle, seemed foolish in comparison. (See I Corinthians 1:22-23.)

For everyone in the first century, Jew and Gentile, the cross was an instrument of torture and execution of criminals. The mention of a cross brought to mind the sight of humiliation, the smell of blood, the cries of agony. To people everywhere, a cross represented pain, condemnation, cruelty, and death.

Preaching about a cross in that day would be like preaching about an electric chair today. Imagine spotting a church building with an electric chair for its visual identification. Or imagine walking into a church to hear the congregation singing "The Old Rugged Hangman's Noose," "Near the Firing Squad," or "Lethal Injection Has Made the Difference for Me." It would certainly seem like a foolish way to attract visitors and make converts.

Paradoxically, God chose the foolishness of preaching, and specifically the seemingly foolish message of the cross, as the means of salvation. He has transformed the cross from an instrument of suffering, punishment, and death into an instrument of healing, deliverance, and eternal life. By the message of the cross, He likewise transforms sinners into saints, blasphemers into missionaries, and persecutors into preachers.

As ministers of the gospel, we should not discount the various means that God uses to draw people to Him, to establish them as disciples, and to provide practical assistance in their everyday lives and relationships. At the same time, we need to recognize that the preaching and teaching of the Word of God is one of the most powerful tools we have. Through our earnest prayer and diligent study of Scripture, God can give us anointed messages of faith, hope, and love that can change individual lives. Apostolic preaching can change our world!

Forward, Summer 2003

CHAPTER 32

Should Every Local Church Have a Senior Pastor?

The standard form of local church government in the United Pentecostal Church International calls for one person to serve as pastor (spiritual leader and overseer), or in a few cases two persons may serve as co-pastors. Since the New Testament speaks of elders in the plural, some have concluded that the leadership of a local congregation should be collective and that no one person should be the senior leader. Which approach is more biblical?

In the Old Testament, we find many examples of teamwork (e.g., Moses and Aaron, Deborah and Barak), delegated authority (e.g., the seventy elders), and mentoring (e.g., Elijah and Elisha). At the same time, God typically anointed senior leaders in charge of significant groups, institutions, and endeavors. Examples are Moses, Joshua, the high priests, the judges, Samuel, the kings, and the prophets.

The New Testament does not provide detailed instructions about church government. Undoubtedly this lack of specificity is intentional, because in God's plan the precise form of church government can vary depending on

215

culture, circumstances, times, and preferences. An organizational form that works in twenty-first-century North America might not work as well in the first-century Middle East or even the twenty-first-century Middle East.

The New Testament does teach us important principles for church government. For instance, we find that the local church is primarily responsible to handle its own affairs under spiritual leadership. At the same time, there is strong emphasis on unity, interdependence, fellowship, ministerial accountability, organization, and structure.

Local churches were led by elders, people whom God calls to the ministry of preaching, teaching, leading, and overseeing the church. In the New Testament, the titles of elder (*presbuteros*, "elder, presbyter"), bishop (*episkopos*, "overseer"), and pastor (*poimen*, "shepherd") are used interchangeably for the spiritual leader of a local congregation. Acts 20:17, 28 says elders (*presbuteros*) are overseers (*episkopos*) and are to feed the church, literally, "to tend as a shepherd" (*poimaino*). Titus 1:5-7 equates elder with bishop. I Peter 5:1-4 describes the work of elders as shepherding the flock (*poimaino*) and taking oversight (*episkopeo*). I Timothy 5:17 similarly describes elders as ruling.

Why does the New Testament speak of "elders" in the plural when describing local churches? We must remember that there were no church buildings in the first century. All believers in a city were considered members of one church, but there was no one building in which all could meet together. Instead, they met in various house churches. In this context, it appears that the elders of the city were the council of leaders of house churches—what we would consider to be pastors of various churches within a city. Another way to view them would be as a ministerial staff or team of a large church.

This explanation reveals how closely the ministers in a city worked together, considering themselves as ministers of one church. From it we can learn some important lessons about unity, mutual accountability, and team leadership. However, nothing in this concept would contradict the idea of a senior pastor or head of the team, which is God's typical plan throughout the Bible. And nothing in this concept would preclude an individual elder from being responsible for a local house meeting. To examine this idea further, let us look at every biblical book that describes the New Testament church in existence (Acts through Revelation).

Acts: While the twelve apostles were the supreme leaders of the church, James the brother of the Lord, who was not one of the Twelve, became the chief elder or senior pastor in Jerusalem. (See Acts 12:17; 15:13; 21:18.)

Romans: Paul mentioned at least three and probably five house churches in Rome with their leaders. (See Romans 16:3-5, 10, 11, 14, 15.) Priscilla and Aquila apparently served as the pastors of the church in their house.

I and II Corinthians: Corinth may fit the model of a council of elders with no strong central leader. However, it was a new church, and it appears that, as the founder, Paul was still functioning as their senior pastor in a transitional phase.

Galatians: This letter was written to a group of churches in a region, so there is no identification of a senior pastor.

217

Ephesians: It was probably a circular letter written first to Ephesus, the capital of the Roman province of Asia, but also meant for the other churches in Asia. (See Acts 19:10, 26.) This could explain why Paul elsewhere referred to a letter to Laodicea (Colossians 4:16), why Ephesians contains no references to individual saints in Ephesus, and why many manuscripts omit the recipients in Ephesians 1:1. If this letter was written to a group of churches, then again, we would not expect mention of an individual pastor.

Philippians: Paul apparently addressed the senior pastor in Philippians 4:3, asking him to mediate a dispute between two female ministers in the church.

Colossians: It seems that Epaphras was the senior pastor (Colossians 1:7), and he was on a trip to Paul at the time, perhaps to discuss the heresy in Colosse against which the letter was written. He also had responsibilities for other churches in the area (Colossians 4:12), so he may have been a regional leader. Nymphas was apparently the pastor of a house church in neighboring Laodicea (Colossians 4:15).

I and II Thessalonians: Paul wrote to the church not long after he founded it, and they still looked to him as their senior pastor (I Thessalonians 2:11, 17).

I and II Timothy: Timothy was the designated leader in Ephesus to help establish the church doctrinally and organizationally (I Timothy 1:3). He was under the authority of the apostle Paul.

Titus: Titus was the designated leader in the island of Crete, charged with organizing churches and ordaining elders in the various communities under his care (Titus 1:5). He was under the authority of the apostle Paul.

Philemon: Philemon had a church in his house in Colosse, and it is likely that Apphia was his wife and Archippus was his son (Philemon 1-2). If so, Archippus may have been the ministerial leader of this house church (Colossians 4:17).

Hebrews, James, I and II Peter, I John, Jude: These are general letters to the church as a whole or to a region or group, so it is not surprising that they would not mention any local pastor.

II and III John: They were written to local churches. It may be that II John 1 addresses a lady pastor, or perhaps John just addressed the church generally. In III John, Gaius and Diotrephes may have been neighboring pastors of house churches, with Diotrephes wrongly trying to assert authority over the whole region or city (Ephesus). In the biblical sense they were members of the same church of the city. Or they could have been leaders who attended the same house church, in which case we see a team leadership under the direction of John, the apostle who had charge of that area as the senior leader.

Revelation: In Revelation 2-3 we find seven letters to the "angels" of seven churches. The Greek word *angelos* literally means "messenger"; this is the alternate translation provided by the NIV. In this context it does not seem possible that they would be spirit beings, because Jesus gave a message to John to transmit to the seven messengers. Would Jesus tell John to write letters to angels rather than Jesus communicating with them directly? If so, why would John need to write in Greek to angelic beings? How would he deliver letters to these angels? What were the angels supposed to do in response to the messages? The messages counsel believers to repent, be

219

faithful, and walk in holiness. How could angels cause human churches to fulfill these admonitions? It seems clear that these seven letters were written to seven individual human messengers whom God held responsible to communicate His Word to their respective churches. In other words, they were the seven senior pastors of seven churches in Asia Minor.

Peter Lampe, professor of New Testament at the University of Heidelberg, Germany, conducted an unprecedented scholarly study of local church organization and government in the first two centuries in Rome, the city for which we can glean the most information. Here is a summary of his findings as excerpted from his book, *From Paul to Valentinus: Christians at Rome in the First Two Centuries* (Minneapolis: Fortress Press, 2003).

"In the pre-Constantine period, the Christians of the city of Rome assembled in premises that were provided by private persons and that were scattered across the city (fractionalization)" (364). Nevertheless, "people writing from outside of Rome could address the Roman Christians as a unity." At the same time, "a plurality of presbyters leads Roman Christianity" (398).

"*All* presbyters are at the same time 'bishops,' and the latter designation specifies one of their special duties. . . . The worship leader always is at the same time also in charge of taking care of the poorer members in his liturgical assembly. *Each* presbyter in Rome apparently leads a worship assembly in a house community and therefore also takes care of needy fellow Christians there. . . . Each individual group was presided over by its own presbyter-bishop" (400).

"For a house community in the second century one has to reckon most probably with only one presbyter. Two or three presbyters for a single house-church community can only be established at the earliest for the third century" (400, n. 8).

"On a level *above* the individual house communities occasional conventions of presbyters took place. . . . All this points to conventions at which the presbyters of the city's individual communities, which acknowledged spiritual fellowship with each other, gathered together" (401).

In summary, we cannot make every detail of twenty-first century UPCI structure conform to first-century church structure, because we do not have enough detail in Scripture to construct a supposed standard model. We have various forms of church government today, within North America as well as overseas, and it seems that there were also various forms in New Testament times. However, we can find evidence in the New Testament for ministerial credentials, recommendations, ministerial discipline, general conferences, home missions programs, foreign missions programs, regional organization, church business meetings and elections, local church discipline, and so on.

We should follow New Testament principles in structuring local, regional, national, and international organization. We need to pay more attention to principles of team leadership and mutual accountability that are often neglected to our hurt. Nevertheless, to implement these principles we should not try to abolish the office of senior pastor of a local church.

Forward, September-October 2005

CHAPTER 33

The Charismatic Ministry of Women in the Early Church

What role should women have in the church today? Historically, Catholic, Orthodox, and Protestant churches have excluded women from public ministry roles, but in today's society many people question this position. To address this issue, it is helpful to study the earliest Christian practices, particularly as revealed in the New Testament.

Based on the historic position of the mainline churches, it may seem that the Bible says little about the possible ministry of women, but we must go beyond traditional analysis if we want information on this subject. In general, traditional historical studies have not adequately addressed the role of women. Joan Scott noted in her chapter on women's history in *New Perspectives on Historical Writing*, "The seemingly modest request that history be supplemented with information about women suggests not only that history as it is is incomplete, but also that historians' mastery of the past is necessarily partial."[1] Despite the possible limitations in source material, we should seek to develop a more complete understanding of early church history.

Women in First-Century Mediterranean Culture

In both Jewish and Greco-Roman society of the first century, women were subordinate to men. There was a strong distinction of gender roles. According to social scientist Bruce Malina, for Americans reading ancient Mediterranean writings the "most distinctive social feature is the gender division. . . . Mediterraneans have a gender-defined society in which gender determines role, rights, obligations, and behavior."[2] Ancient Mediterraneans made clear distinctions between male and female with regard to "place, object, task, and time." For example, with regard to space, "males live in the public ('open') area of fields, marketplaces, and the like; females in the private ('covered') world of houses, wells, common ovens, and the like."[3] Malina further explained:

> It is a matter of honor and praise that each gender keeps to its own gender-specific tasks. . . . It is impossible to overestimate the importance of honor and shame in the socialization of males and females in the ancient Mediterranean world. . . . To know the gender of someone was already to know a whole set of norms to which they must conform if they were to be honorable in that society. Such expectations formed clear cultural norms about what clothes (Deut. 22:5), hairdos (1 Cor. 11:4-14), and sexual partners (Rom. 1:26-27) are appropriate to males and females.[4]

Halvor Moxnes likewise explains that "honor and shame" were central components of the common Mediterranean culture of the first century, and honor and shame were strongly associated with "sexual roles and gender division."[5] Honor was achieved by acting in accordance with societal norms for one's gender, while shame accrued to those who violated those norms. For the most part, public leadership was considered to be masculine, so that a man who exhibited leadership qualities was honored. By contrast, it was generally considered shameful for a woman to step outside her societal and familial boundaries to assert public authority, and it was generally considered shameful for a man to submit to such feminine authority. As a result, Ross Kraemer notes, women had little opportunity for public leadership in the area of religion:

> For the vast majority of women in Greco-Roman antiquity, gender . . . imposed all sorts of limitations on their lives. Gender constrained women's participation in public life (social, political, and religious). . . . All this was true for most Jewish women as well. . . . Yet, we have also seen that in diverse Jewish communities in the Greco-Roman diaspora, Jewish women were active participants in communal life, contributing financial resources and serving as synagogue officers and benefactors.[6]

Some feminists do not like to cite this evidence of the limitations on women, on the ground that we should not disparage Jewish or pagan religion of the first century.[7] However, while it is possible to exaggerate the contrast between early Christian practice and pagan and Jewish practice in the first century, it is also possible to underestimate it. The fact remains that women are far more prominent in the New Testament than one would expect simply by studying its cultural and social environment. It appears that for at least "some of the early Christian communities," as well as the Greco-Roman mysteries, "the membership and leadership . . . were more open and egalitarian than the public cults [religions]."[8]

The Prominent Role of Women in the New Testament

When we look for evidence of women's ministry in the New Testament, we find significant information that is often overlooked. Bart Ehrman summarized the evidence as follows:

> Women played a prominent role in the earliest Christian churches, including those associated with the apostle Paul. They served as evangelists, pastors, teachers, and prophets. Some were wealthy and provided financial support for the apostles; others served as patrons for entire churches, allowing congregations to meet in their homes and supplying them with the resources necessary for their gatherings. Some women were Paul's co-workers on the mission field.[9]

Some who oppose public ministry for women minimize this evidence and instead point to other material in the New Testament that may seem to limit women's roles. Some feminists similarly argue that the New Testament is overwhelmingly patriarchal and does not give strong support for women's ministry; they reject its authority.[10] Many theologians conclude that the New

Testament contains conflicting messages.

Does the New Testament contradict itself on the subject of women in ministry? Were the earliest Christian churches in conflict on this issue? Must we choose one side or the other and dismiss contrary evidence or practice? Or can we find a consistent pattern for women's ministry in the early church—one that accounts for all the evidence?

To answer these questions, we will examine the role of women in the early church, looking particularly at women in the Gospels and Acts, in the ministry and teaching of Paul, and in early Christianity after the New Testament. We conclude that women did have public ministry roles in the early church and that the early church in general had a consistent position on women in ministry.

Evidence from the Gospels and Acts

All four Gospels speak of women as some of the most faithful followers of Jesus. For example, women from Galilee came to Jerusalem for the final week of Jesus' life and were present at his crucifixion, even when the apostles fled.[11] Moreover, women were the first to proclaim the resurrection of Jesus, which is what makes the gospel the "good news."[12] That all four Gospels record the prominent role of the women disciples of Jesus indicates that this information does not come to us because of the redactional emphasis of one author but must be deeply embedded in the original historical events as well as the earliest traditions of the church.

The Synoptic Gospels tell the story of several notable women who are characterized by having greater faith or discernment than those around them, even including the male disciples:

- The woman with a hemorrhage (Mark 5:25-34).
  She had faith to touch Jesus for healing, even
  though the disciples did not understand the significance of Jesus' statement that someone had
  touched him (in a way that led to a miracle).
- The woman who anointed Jesus' feet shortly before
  his death (Mark 14:3-9). The Gospel presents her
  as intuitively understanding that the time of his
  death was drawing near, in contrast to the disciples.
- The Syro-Phoenician woman who exhibited great
  faith even though she was not a Jew and was not in
  the target audience of Jesus' ministry at that time
  (Matthew 15:21-28; Mark 7:24-30). In the words of
  Elisabeth Schüssler Fiorenza, "The Syro-Phoenician woman . . . has become the apostolic
  'foremother' of all Gentile Christians."[13]

Matthew's genealogy of Jesus draws attention to four
women who transcended immoral or pagan backgrounds
to become ancestors in the family of Jesus: Tamar, Rahab,
Ruth, and the wife of Uriah (Bathsheba) (Matthew 1:3, 5,
6). It was unusual for a Jewish genealogy to mention
women, especially those of questionable backgrounds.
The indication is that God can use women, even sinful
women, to advance God's purpose if they submit to the
divine will.

Mark contains a strong statement about the importance of the women disciples: "There were also women
looking on from afar, among whom were Mary Magdalene, Mary the mother of James the Less and of Joses,
and Salome, who also followed Him and ministered to
Him when He was in Galilee, and many other women who

came up with Him to Jerusalem" (Mark 15:40-41). (Biblical quotations are from the NKJV.) In this passage, "followed" is from *akoloutheō* with the connotation of "to follow as a disciple." "Ministered" is from *diakoneō*, here referring to financial support but possibly having a broader significance. Mary Rose D'Angelo explained:

> The Greek word is *diēkonoun*, which means "wait on table, serve," and through the New Testament, but especially in Mark, "minister." W. D. Davies has argued that the word group *diakon-* is the Greek equivalent of a Hebrew term used to denote special disciples, who are close personal attendants, apprentices, and heirs of the teacher, like Joshua to Moses. He attributes this meaning to the verb in 15:41.[14]

It is generally acknowledged that Luke drew attention to the role of women. Some say that he did so to elevate their status, while others argue that he did so for the apologetic purpose of showing that Christian women adhered to societal norms, i.e., kept their place. But even if the latter were true, the perceived need for an apologetic reveals that Christian women had a prominent role that could cause nonbelievers to question the early church.

Luke describes Elizabeth as giving prophecy and identifies Anna as a prophetess (Luke 1:41-45; 2:36). Like Mark, Luke identifies several women who were prominent disciples and financial supporters of Jesus: "Now it came to pass, afterward, that He went through every city and village, preaching and bringing the glad tidings of the kingdom of God. And the twelve were with Him, and certain women who had been healed of evil spirits and infirmities—Mary called Magdalene, out of whom had come seven demons, and Joanna the wife of Chuza, Herod's steward, and Susanna, and many others who provided for Him from their substance" (Luke 8:1-3). Here, "provided" is from *diakoneō*, the same word used in Mark 15:41 for "ministered."

John devotes most of chapter 4 to a Samaritan woman. Despite her sinful background and outsider status, she became one of the first people to recognize Jesus as the Messiah and one of the first to witness to others about him. Because of her testimony, many people believed on Jesus, even though the male disciples did not realize the opportunity to share truth with her or the townspeople. Similarly, over half of chapter 20, the climax of John, deals with Mary Magdalene. She was the first person to see the resurrected Christ and the first to witness of his resurrection—literally, the first evangelist, or bearer of the good news.

Near the beginning of Acts there is a powerful affirmation of the ministry of women, quoted from Joel and included in the inaugural sermon of the apostle Peter on the birthday of the church: "'And it shall come to pass in the last days,' says God, 'that I will pour out of My Spirit on all flesh; your sons and your daughters shall prophesy, your young men shall see visions, your old men shall dream dreams. And on My menservants and on My maidservants I will pour out My Spirit in those days; and they shall prophesy'" (Acts 2:17-18). Prominent women disciples in Acts include:

- Lydia, a dealer of purple cloth in Philippi and head

of household (Acts 16:13-15). She hosted Paul's
missionary team in her house.

- Priscilla (Acts 18:2, 18-19, 26), always mentioned
along with her husband, Aquila, for they evidently
formed a ministerial team. Remarkably, she is mentioned before her husband in two of three places,
which implies that she had the leading role in ministry. She and her husband accompanied Paul to
Syria and Ephesus to assist him in missionary
work. Together they taught Apollos, an outstanding
preacher, and brought him into the New Testament
church.
- Four daughters of Philip the evangelist who were
prophetesses: "This man had four virgin daughters
who prophesied" (Acts 21:9).

Mary Rose D'Angelo concludes that Mark and John
"assume the participation of women in communal life in
ways that would cause dissension" and "offer at least
some vivid and dynamic representations of women." She
attributed this to two factors: (1) "the continued importance of prophetic experience" with leadership
depending "on a call based in spiritual experience rather
than on appointment"; and (2) the identification of
church life with "the private and voluntary sphere."[15]

D'Angelo further notes that Matthew accepts "the
continued communal and prophetic activity of women, as
Mark and John do." Moreover, "the author of Luke-Acts
appears to have deliberately multiplied representations
of women within the narrative. . . . Unlike the other three
canonical gospels, Luke-Acts uses gender as a central
category." At the same time, she points out that some
feminists believe that Luke-Acts restricts or denigrates

women because it depicts Christian women as "properly behaved. Male and female roles are clearly and appropriately delineated."[16]

Elisabeth Schüssler Fiorenza agrees that Luke-Acts puts women in a subordinate role but argues that we can nevertheless find evidence in Luke-Acts of a liberating role for women. She accepts the theory that in order to present Christianity as respectable in ancient society, "Luke attempts to mute the 'radical' traditions of the Jesus movement that ascribe to women, the poor, and the outcast a significant role." Nevertheless, she suggests "that we read Luke's work in terms of both the liberationist and the adaptationist argument. Such a reading recognizes the submerged traditions which are inscribed in the text."[17]

In summary, the Gospels depict women among the foremost disciples and ascribe to them great faith, discernment, and loyalty, equal to or exceeding that of the most prominent male disciples. Women were effective evangels and in fact were the first to proclaim the resurrection of Jesus. They are not pictured as flouting societal norms, however, or displacing the apostles. Nevertheless, there is at least the implication that women can be as fully capable as men with respect to all the essential attributes and functions of a disciple.

In Acts, we find explicit endorsement of the charismatic ministry of women. Apparently the top institutional leadership was male—as in the twelve original apostles of Acts 1 and the seven original deacons of Acts 6 (if indeed these men are to be considered deacons). Nevertheless, we find women as missionaries, teachers, prophetesses, and patrons of local churches.

Evidence from the Pauline Epistles

Evidence from the Pauline Epistles further establishes the important position of women in the early church. Paul and the Pauline community spoke of women leaders as ministers or deacons. Let us particularly examine the women ministers mentioned in Romans 16.

In verse 1, Paul called Phoebe a "servant" (KJV, NKJV), "deacon" (NRSV), or "minister" (NRSV note) of the church at Cenchreae, indicating that she had some official ministerial role in that local assembly. "I commend to you Phoebe our sister, who is a servant of the church in Cenchrea, that you may receive her in the Lord in a manner worthy of the saints, and assist her in whatever business she has need of you; for indeed she has been a helper of many and of myself also" (Romans 16:1-2, NKJV).

In Greek her title is *diakonos* meaning "servant, helper, minister; deacon; deaconess."[18] In Philippians 1:1 and I Timothy 3:8, 12, the major translations render this word as "deacon."

After I Timothy 3:8-10 presents the qualifications of deacons, verse 11 begins to discuss the qualifications of some women. It uses the plural of the word *gynē*. The basic meaning of this word is "woman"; it can be used of any adult female or specifically of a wife.[19] The NRSV notes that in the context it may refer to "their [deacons'] wives" or to "women deacons." Raymond Brown has concluded:

> Probably there are also women deacons. . . .
> After a treatment of male deacons in 3:8-10, the next verse begins "Women also." Grammar strongly favors the interpretation that this means

"women (who are deacons)" rather than "women (wives of deacons)." The wife of the deacon is mentioned as a distinct role in 3:12.[20]

The New Testament also uses the word *diakonos* of Christ, Paul, Apollos, Epaphras, Timothy, and Tychicus.[21] With this usage in mind, Edith Castelli has argued that for Phoebe "minister" is a more appropriate translation than "deacon":

> Translators routinely render the Greek term *diakonos* as "minister" in English when the Greek term refers to one of the many Christian men who taught, preached, rendered a variety of spiritual services to newly formed Christian communities, and possessed an ample amount of authority and leadership status within such communities.[22]

Elisabeth Schüssler Fiorenza similarly concluded that "Phoebe is recommended as an official teacher and missionary in the church of Cenchreae."[23]

Paul also spoke of Phoebe as a helper or benefactor, *prostatis*, of the church in Cenchrea (Romans 16:2). This word appears only here in the New Testament, and it means "protectress, patroness, helper."[24] The verb form, *proistēmi*, means to "be a leader, have authority over, manage; care for, give help; engage in, practice."[25] Clearly, it refers to some leadership role in the local church.[26]

Next Paul told the Roman church, "Greet Priscilla and Aquila, my fellow workers in Christ Jesus, who risked their own necks for my life, to whom not only I give thanks, but also all the churches of the Gentiles. Likewise greet the church that is in their house" (Romans 16:3-5, NKJV). From Acts, we learn that they traveled as missionaries with Paul and instructed the noted preacher Apollos. Here we learn that they hosted a church in their house, no doubt leading that home church as the equivalent of local pastors. Priscilla is mentioned first, since she was apparently the foremost minister of the pair. I Corinthians 16:19 and II Timothy 4:19 also name the couple; overall, Priscilla is mentioned first in four of six places in the New Testament.

In Romans 16:3, Paul spoke of Priscilla and Aquila as fellow workers, *synergos*, which functions almost as a title for a gospel preacher. Elsewhere he used this word for Urbanus, Timothy, Apollos, Titus, Epaphroditus, Clement, Aristarchus, Mark, Jesus Justus, Philemon, Demas, and Luke.[27] Bauer et al. noted, "Paul refers to those who helped him in spreading the gospel as *his fellow-workers*."[28]

In Romans 16:7, Paul wrote, "Greet Andronicus and Junia, my countrymen and my fellow prisoners, who are of note among the apostles, who also were in Christ before me" (NKJV). Here he identified a man and a woman, probably a married couple like Priscilla and Aquila, as apostles. While it is possible to interpret the phrase as meaning that they were well-known to the apostles, the more natural reading is that they were well-known as apostles. In the New Testament, the term "apostle" identifies a larger category than the original twelve, including such people as Paul, Barnabas, and James the Lord's brother. Literally meaning someone sent with a commission, it refers to significant leaders and missionaries.

There is some question about the name Junia. The Greek text has *Iounian*, in the accusative case. This word could be masculine or feminine, depending on the accent. *'Iouniân* (circumflex accent over the alpha) is masculine, referring to the name Junias; *'Iounían* (acute accent over the iota) is feminine, referring to the name Junia. Some manuscripts have the masculine form, while others have the feminine. The masculine form seems doubtful because Junia was a common female name, while Junias was unknown. The Chester Beatty Papyri have the similar feminine name *'Ioulían*, and so do some Old Latin, Coptic, and Ethiopian manuscripts. The traditional text (KJV, NKJV) and the current scholarly text (United Bible Societies, 4th ed., and Nestle-Aland, 27th ed.) both choose the feminine name Junia.

Thus, most ancient commentators interpreted the name as Junia and held that she was the wife of Andronicus. In the fourth century John Chrysostom remarked, "Oh! how great is the devotion of this woman, that she should be even counted worthy of the appellation of apostle!"[29]

Bauer et al. explained that in the New Testament and early Christian literature the Greek name is "not found elsewh., prob. short form of the common Junianus. . . . The possibility, fr. a purely lexical point of view, that this is a woman's name 'Iounía . . . (ancient commentators took Andr. and Junia as a married couple . . .) deserves consideration."[30]

Among major translations, the KJV, NKJV, NRSV, and NLT translate the name as Junia (feminine). The RSV, NIV, and NASB translate the name as Junias (masculine). Margaret MacDonald stated of the name Junias:

This supposedly masculine name never occurs in ancient literature, and the earliest Christian interpreters of New Testament texts (commonly known as the Church Fathers) took the name to be feminine. . . . Some have proposed that Andronicus and Junia may have been prominent among the apostles in the sense that they were valued by apostles, but without actually being apostles themselves. Although this interpretation is possible based on the Greek text, the most straightforward reading is to understand Paul as calling both Andronicus and Junia apostles.[31]

Paul mentioned several other women gospel workers in the following verses: "Greet Mary, who labored much for us. . . . Greet Tryphena and Tryphosa, who have labored in the Lord. Greet the beloved Persis, who labored much in the Lord. Greet Rufus, chosen in the Lord, and his mother and mine. . . . Greet Philologus and Julia, Nereus and his sister, and Olympas, and all the saints who are with them" (Romans 16:6, 12-13, 15, NKJV). For Mary, Tryphaena, Tryphosa, and Persis, he used the word *kopiaō*, meaning "labor." The same word is used of Paul's own ministry[32] and the ministry of other leaders.[33]

Other epistles of Paul also mention some prominent women:

- Chloe was the head of a household in Corinth and sent a delegation to Paul from the church there (I Corinthians 1:11).
- Paul's letter to Philemon was also addressed to Apphia, probably Philemon's wife (Philemon 2).

- In Philippians 4:2-3 Paul wrote concerning two prominent women in the church, "I implore Euodia and I implore Syntyche to be of the same mind in the Lord. And I urge you also, true companion, help these women who labored with me in the gospel, with Clement also, and the rest of my fellow workers, whose names are in the Book of Life" (NKJV). Verse 3 speaks of these women as *synergos*, fellow worker, again denoting a leadership role.
- Colossians 4:15 possibly speaks of a woman who was the leader of a house church. "Give my greetings to the brothers at Laodicea, and to Nympha and the church in her house" (NIV). Although the KJV and NKJV use the masculine name Nymphas, the NIV and NRSV use the feminine name Nympha, which appears in the critical text. Margaret MacDonald commented, "It is now widely recognized that the attempt to masculinize Nympha, which appears in several ancient versions of the text . . . is rooted in the scandal created by the existence of a woman leader of a house-church."[34]

Bruce Malina has offered an explanation of how women could have achieved such prominent church positions in a society where gender roles were so distinct. In first-century Mediterranean culture, groups "are gender assessed." Some groups "are on the mother's side or are run by persons without legal rights (e.g., early Christian churches). . . . Some places are distinctively female: for example, the inside of a house."[35] Since the earliest Christian churches met in homes, and since homes were places where women were culturally able to provide leadership, early Christian women could fill leadership and ministry roles.

Regardless of the exact cultural explanation, the Pauline Epistles show that women exercised considerable leadership in the early church, contrary to the situation in later church history. In the words of Schüssler Fiorenza, "Women as well as men were traveling missionaries and leaders of house-churches."[36]

New Testament Teaching on Women in Ministry
Now let us briefly examine the major didactic passages in the New Testament that discuss the role of women in the church: (1) the egalitarian statement of Galatians 3:28; (2) the household codes in Ephesians 5 and Colossians 3; (3) the teaching on gender distinction in I Corinthians 11, (4) the instructions for church services in I Corinthians 14; and (5) the statement on women in authority in I Timothy 2.

Galatians. Galatians 3:28 is a broad and strong statement of the equality of all Christians: "There is neither Jew nor Greek, there is neither slave nor free, there is neither male nor female; for you are all one in Christ Jesus" (NKJV). It does not appear that these distinctions were abolished in the daily life of believers. For instance, Galatians 2 indicates that the early church used two different approaches for reaching Jews and Gentiles. They expected that Jewish believers would continue to be circumcised while recognizing that a Gentile such as Titus did not need to be circumcised. As the household codes show, they also thought that men and women should have distinct roles in the family. Nevertheless, all believers, regardless of social distinctions, have equal privileges and status in the church of God. In dealing with human social structures there might well remain differences, but there is no difference with respect to the grace and gifts of God—which would certainly include charismatic ministry and leadership.

Ephesians and Colossians. In Ephesians 5 and Colossians 3, we find instructions for the operation of a Christian household, patterned after similar household codes in secular first-century Roman literature. These passages establish the husband as the head of the household and instruct the wife to follow his godly leadership. Likewise they tell children to obey parents and slaves or servants to obey masters as part of the temporal order.

At first glance, it may seem that these passages simply uphold traditional societal norms. However, something different is going on, for the instructions are based on an inherent equality among believers. For instance, in God's sight, slaves and masters are equal (Ephesians 6:9). Similarly, immediately before the discussion of the roles of husband and wife, Ephesians 5:21 enunciates the principle of mutual submission. James Hollingshead has concluded that, while Roman society influenced Paul's letters, Paul also critiqued the prevailing social order in two ways. First, his instructions partly violate the traditional hierarchical structure of the Roman household by conferring membership and status to those considered subordinate. Second, his Christian worldview was egalitarian. "Paul's communities included—as apparent equals—slaves, women, freedmen, and perhaps even some prominent free men."[37]

Hollingshead maintains that although Paul taught Christians to live in an orderly fashion with respect for diversity of roles, he did not simply embrace social conventions but in fact subverted them with a new form of organization. Instead of building the church on social hierarchies, he wanted it to function as a body in which all members are equally valued. He sought to reconcile differences into unity or community. By describing the church as the body of Christ, instead of a household, he critiqued traditional ideas of hierarchy. Hollingshead concludes that Paul treated "women as equals and patrons, and argue[d] that slaves should be freed," and considered the gospel to be "the favorable proclamation that all peoples could live together as clients of God."[38]

I Corinthians 11. Paul taught that the roles of men and women are distinct, and they should signify this distinction by their outward appearance. He assumed that women would be involved in public worship and ministry, but he instructed them not to use this involvement to abolish legitimate social distinctions. Again, these instructions assume an inherent equality and interdependence of male and female (I Corinthians 11:8-12).

Hollingshead concludes that prophetesses in the Corinthian church were imitating the priestesses of Isis by wearing their hair down while prophesying and that Paul opposed this practice because it violated women's proper role. He did not restrict the rights of women, but he opposed the women in Corinth who claimed a special spiritual status that allowed them to violate the established distinctions between male and female.

> Paul here insists that a distinction between the sexes should remain. What is often missed, however, is the fact that Paul *expects the Corinthians to agree with him.* An "argument from shame" is useless if the audience is proud of

the very thing that is supposed to shame them. . . .

What angers Paul is not the fact that women carry out roles in worship; he assumes as much in 11:5 without comment. What angers him is the assignation of special cultic status to any member of the community, whether male or female. Men and women are different, and Paul thinks that these differences are natural, the product of the intention of God (11:9, 14). But whatever the differences between individuals, whether differences of gender or of spiritual gifts, no one in the community can claim to be set apart, no *one* can claim a higher knowledge, a greater wisdom, access to a deeper mystery of Christ.[39]

Regardless of Hollingshead's understanding of the particular situation in Corinth, his basic point is well taken: Paul supported the ministry of women but wanted them to exercise their ministry in a distinctively feminine manner that would be appropriate to the created order. Specifically, he wanted them to have long hair as a distinctive mark of femininity. (The Greek word *komaō* means "wear long hair, let one's hair grow long."[40]) Ehrman concluded:

Paul maintained that there was still to be a difference between men and women in this world. To eradicate that difference, in Paul's view, was unnatural and wrong. . . . It is quite clear from Paul's arguments that women could and did participate openly in the church alongside men—but they were to do so as women, not as men.[41]

I Corinthians 14. Here we have a passage that seems to place some limitation on the participation of women in public worship: "Let your women keep silent in the churches, for they are not permitted to speak; but they are to be submissive, as the law also says. And if they want to learn something, let them ask their own husbands at home; for it is shameful for women to speak in church" (I Corinthians 14:34-35, NKJV).[42]

Traditionally, this passage has been interpreted to mean that women should not preach or teach in public worship. This interpretation does not fit the immediate context, however, or the larger context of the Pauline corpus. The rest of chapter 14 emphasizes that "all" may participate in charismatic utterances in public worship, such as tongues and prophecy. "For you can all prophesy one by one" (I Corinthians 14:31, NKJV). "All" may prophesy (verses 5, 24), and it is possible that "each of you has a psalm, has a teaching, has a tongue, has a revelation, has an interpretation" (verse 26, NKJV). Earlier in the letter, Paul plainly assumed that both men and women would pray and prophesy in public worship and simply instructed that they maintain a symbolic distinction of gender when doing so. "Every man praying or prophesying, having his head covered, dishonors his head. But every woman who prays or prophesies with her head uncovered dishonors her head, for that is one and the same as if her head were shaved" (I Corinthians 11:4-5, NKJV). And, as we have seen, Paul had numerous women co-workers in the gospel.

Consequently, Gordon Fee has argued that verses 34-35 are not part of the original text: "The case against these verses is so strong, and finding a viable solution to their meaning so difficult, that it seems best to view them as an interpolation."[43] Bart Ehrman concurred: "However the verses came to be placed into the text, it does not appear that they were written by Paul but by someone living later."[44] This view is a minority one, however, because textual evidence of interpolation is lacking. All the major manuscripts contain these verses, including the Chester Beatty Papyri, Sinaiticus, Alexandrinus, and Vaticanus, although a few place them after verse 40, including Bezae, Cambridge, and Dresden.[45]

A related idea has been advanced by Paul Achtemeier, Joel Green, and Marianne Meye Thompson. While regarding the text as original, they conclude that verses 34-35 are merely quoted from Corinthian believers, while in verse 36 Paul refuted the idea they expressed:

> In verse 36, the word translated "only ones" is, in the Greek text, masculine! That means Paul has addressed this condemnation not to women, but to men! The Greek makes clear that it is men who act as though they alone should be allowed to speak, and it is to them that this rebuke is addressed. It is therefore evident that what Paul does here is what he regularly does in this letter: in 14:33b-35 he quotes what some Corinthian Christians have been saying, and then refutes it. . . . Paul is therefore not telling women that they are not to participate fully in worship; he has already assumed that they will do so (11:4-5). He is telling the men who apparently want to restrict women, the men whom he quotes verses 33b-35, that such an attitude is not to be tolerated since

they, the men, did not originate God's word, and
that they are therefore not the only ones to whom
God's word has come.[46]

A study of the literary and sociological context, however, indicates that the words can be understood as part of
the original text and as the teaching of Paul himself. In I
Corinthians 14, Paul dealt with order in public worship.
Immediately before verses 34-35, he gave guidelines for the
orderly conduct of public worship services, including the
proper use of teaching, tongues, interpretation of tongues,
and prophecy (verses 26-33). He sought to curb specific
imbalances or abuses in the Corinthian church that were
causing disruption and confusion (verses 23, 33). Paul did
not thereby disparage the use of tongues and prophecy, but
commended their use as long as it was orderly and beneficial to the whole assembly (verses 13-18, 39-40).

In this context, it is best to view verses 34-35 as a
similar regulation of potentially disruptive utterances in
public worship. Paul did not deny or disparage the ministry of women, but he sought to correct certain abuses
involving women that caused disorder.

What were the abuses in the Corinthian church
involving women? The text does not say specifically,
although the Corinthians would have been well aware of
them, but there is a clue in verse 35: "If they want to
learn something, let them ask their own husbands at
home." The problem involved situations in which the congregation was supposed to listen to a teacher, yet some
women were disorderly. Apparently, these women were
calling out questions during the teaching. This practice
was disruptive, and the solution was for them to ask the

questions of their husbands privately.

Why were the questions from women so disruptive? First, it is probable that men and women were separated in church services, for in the first century generally women were seated separately from men in social functions.[47] "Gender-segregated public seating was by no means unknown in Greco-Roman antiquity and is, in fact, well attested for everything from the theater to Christian churches."[48] Second, most women were not as educated as men, and thus were less likely to understand points in public discourse. Reading was taught to "male citizens, slaves trained as pedagogues for children of the elite, retainers (scribes, secretaries, some government and religious officials) of the elite class, some upper-class Greek and more upper-class Roman women"; generally speaking, Jewish women were not literate.[49]

In short, it appears that during public teaching, many Corinthian women did not fully understand the lesson and called out questions to their husbands, who were seated separately from them, or perhaps even called out questions to the speaker (a privilege that males had in Greco-Roman culture). This practice was noisy and disruptive. The command to "be submissive" indicates that the public questioning by the women was viewed as disrespectful or challenging of authority. Thus, Paul instructed the women to be quiet during the teaching and to be respectful of male authority. But nothing he said prohibits women from addressing the whole congregation under the anointing of the Holy Spirit.

I Timothy 2. "Let a woman learn in silence with all submission. And I do not permit a woman to teach or to have authority over a man, but to be in silence. For Adam was formed first, then Eve. And Adam was not deceived, but the woman being deceived, fell into transgression. Nevertheless she will be saved in childbearing if they continue in faith, love, and holiness, with self-control" (I Timothy 2:11-15, NKJV). This passage is similar to I Corinthians 14, and while it makes a more general statement, we should read it in a similar cultural and historical light. We should not interpret it in isolation from the rest of the New Testament.

In verses 11 and 12, "silence" and "be in silence" come from the word *hēsuchia*, which means "silence, quietness."[50] The same word appears in II Thessalonians 3:12: "Now those who are such we command and exhort through our Lord Jesus Christ that they work in quietness and eat their own bread" (NKJV). By definition and in context, this word does not indicate absolute silence (unlike *sigē* in Revelation 8:1), but it speaks of the proper attitude of quietness, reverence, and careful attention in public worship. We might well contrast it to the disruption in the Corinthian church.

In verse 12, the word translated "have authority over" is *authenteō*, and it appears in the New Testament only here. The meaning is to "domineer, have authority over."[51] Thus, a woman should not become the authoritative teacher of men in general and should not try to dominate men.

Verses 13-14 appeal to the Old Testament to establish the principle of male leadership. The key point from Genesis is that men should not abandon their responsibility of leadership (which Adam did) and women should not usurp the male role (which Eve did).

Does I Timothy 2:11-15 teach that Paul's female co-workers were in violation of God's principle of authority?

There is no need to draw this conclusion, for these women ministered under the authority of the church and its received tradition from the male apostles, and they also ministered under the authority of the apostle Paul himself. In this connection, Raymond Brown noted that the passage may specifically warn against a woman who would proclaim a different doctrine than what the church had already approved:

> Yet there has been support recently for another way of interpreting this passage against the background of the letter's attack on false teaching. . . . Thus, not women in general but women who became the spokespersons of the error to which they had been enticed would have been the object of the prohibition of teaching and holding authority.[52]

Early Post-Biblical Evidence

Although we can only briefly touch on the evidence, sources from the second and third century reveal that women continued to serve as leaders and ministers in the early Christian church.

In the mid second century, Montanus founded a movement that emphasized gifts of the Spirit, the priesthood of believers, and personal holiness. He had two prominent female assistants, Priscilla and Maximilla, and according to Hippolytus, the Montanists accepted them as "prophetesses." Hippolytus criticized, "They magnify these wretched women above the Apostles and every gift of Grace."[53] According to Paul Johnson, "Montanism, or rather the efforts to combat it, played a conclusive role in persuading the orthodox to ban the ministry to women."[54]

The Acts of Paul and Thecla is a second-century imaginative account of a prominent woman. Facing what seemed to be imminent death, Thecla baptized herself "in the name of Jesus Christ." After she was delivered from death, Paul accepted her baptism as valid. When she told him she planned to go to Iconium, Paul replied, "Go and teach the word of God."[55] While there is no historical basis for this story, it reveals contemporary attitudes about the role of women.

In the early third century, some women were both teaching and baptizing, and some cited Thecla as precedent. Tertullian opposed this practice on the basis of I Corinthians 14:34-35.[56]

The *Didascalia Apostolorum* (third century) recognizes deaconesses, and ancient Christian inscriptions from about the same time refer to women deacons and even elders (presbyters). As Francine Cardman noted, "It is difficult to know with any certainty what these titles mean in regard to any of the women, but it is worth considering that they mean what they say."[57]

From this brief survey, we find women prophetesses, preachers, teachers, deaconesses, and elders in the second and third centuries. While they apparently exercised their ministries under the overall male leadership of the church, they were recognized as leaders themselves. This evidence corresponds closely to what we find in the New Testament itself.

In subsequent centuries, the role of women greatly diminished. Women could no longer serve as deacons and elders, preachers and teachers. Our survey has hinted at some possible reasons why. First, when the church was officially endorsed and church buildings were erected, the church moved from the home, where the role of women was respected, into the public arena, where men were dominant. Second, an overreaction to Montanism and to heretical teachings of women may have caused a curtailing of women's ministry. Third, as the church became more institutionalized and formalized, it began to lose its emphasis on spiritual gifts and the priesthood of all believers—thus the rise of Montanism as a restorationist movement. Since the ministry of women was closely connected to, and justified by, the anointing of the Spirit rather than cultural norms, when charismatic ministry declined and disappeared so did the ministry of women.

Conclusions

1. *Women filled leadership and public ministry roles in the early church.* The church accepted their ministry not because it conformed to societal norms but because it stemmed from "the gifts and the calling of God" (Romans 11:29, NKJV) and "the manifestation of the Spirit . . . given to each one for the profit of all" (I Corinthians 12:7, NKJV). Women's ministry was not institutional but charismatic.

2. *At the same time, the early church did not seek to overthrow the traditional societal role of women as distinct from that of men.* The church taught that in the family, the church, and society, men and women had distinct roles that should not be blurred or crossed and that this basic distinction was ordained by God in creation. Thus Edith Castelli explained:

Paul is quite concerned with the careful maintenance of gender differences in appearance (justified in part by the . . . argument that "nature" affirms the conventional practice of men wearing their hair short and women wearing their hair long) not simply because he thinks it is a good idea, but because he thinks that the created order demands it. . . . Like 1 Cor 11:2-16, Rom 1:18-32 interweaves its indictment of a particular human practice with theological propositions. Both texts argue that the human behavior in question—whether it be abandoning conventionally gender-linked appearance and dress (in general or in certain contexts) or engaging in certain apparently non-normative sexual practices—is a violation of a worldly order that is grounded in a cosmically, divinely willed order. Gender differences, according to these texts, are not the mere fruits of social conventions, but are God given and divinely warranted.[58]

3. *In the New Testament churches overall, the charismatic ministry of women and the distinct social role of women were held in balance.* Thus in I Corinthians 11, Paul expected women to pray and prophesy in public worship and yet still retain a distinctively feminine appearance. In I Corinthians 14, Paul expected that all believers, including women, could prophesy or teach in public worship and yet expected women to be respectful listeners when others spoke.

4. *After the New Testament, however, as ministry became less charismatic and more institutional,*

concepts of ministry gradually conformed to social and cultural norms. Women continued to have some public ministry roles for several centuries, but eventually these opportunities were withdrawn.

In summary, the New Testament gives significant guidance on the subject of women in ministry. Churches that consider the Bible as authoritative do not need to embrace radical feminist deconstruction in order to acknowledge the role of women in ministry. Instead, by adopting a more charismatic, less institutional understanding of ministerial calling, gifts, and anointing, they can make room for women in ministry while still maintaining biblical norms for marriage and the family.

The first-century church gave a far greater role to women than one might suppose from a study of first-century Mediterranean culture. If churches today embrace the values of the New Testament, then they must confront a history that has not generally been supportive of women in ministry. The words of Karlyn Kohrs Campbell issue a challenge: "The rhetoric of women's liberation appeals to what are said to be shared moral values, but forces recognition that those values are not shared, thereby creating the most intense of moral conflicts."[59]

Those who value charismatic ministry—ministry in the power of the Holy Spirit—should value the ministry of women of the Spirit.

Notes

[1]Joan W. Scott, "Women's History," pages 43-70 in *New Perspectives on Historical Writing*, 2d ed. (ed. Peter Burke; University Park, Pa.: Pennsylvania State University Press, 2001), 52.

[2]Bruce Malina, "Understanding New Testament Persons," in *The Social Sciences and New Testament Interpretation* (ed. Richard

Rohrbaugh; Peabody, Mass.: Hendrickson, 1996), 49-51.

[3]Bruce Malina and Jerome Neyrey, *Portraits of Paul: An Archaeology of Ancient Personality* (Louisville: Westminster John Knox, 1996), 104-5.

[4]Ibid., 178, 182.

[5]Halvor Moxnes, "Honor and Shame," in *Social Sciences*, 25.

[6]Ross S. Kraemer, "Jewish Women and Women's Judaism(s) at the Beginning of Christianity," in *Women & Christian Origins* (eds. Ross Kraemer and Mary D'Angelo; New York: Oxford University Press, 1999), 72.

[7]Elisabeth Schüssler Fiorenza, *But She Said: Feminist Practices of Biblical Interpretation* (Boston: Beacon, 1992), 59.

[8]Lynn R. LiDonnici, "Women's Religions and Religious Lives in the Greco-Roman City," in *Women & Christian Origins*, 97.

[9]Bart D. Ehrman, *The New Testament: A Historical Introduction to the Early Christian Writings*, 2d ed. (New York: Oxford University Press, 2000).

[10]Schüssler Fiorenza, *But She Said*, 37, 50, 137, 193.

[11]Matthew 27:55; Mark 15:40-41; Luke 23:49, 55; John 19:25.

[12]Matthew 28:1-10; Mark 16:1-8; Luke 23:55-24:10; John 20:1-2.

[13]Elisabeth Schüssler Fiorenza, *In Memory of Her: A Feminist Theological Reconstruction of Christian Origins* (New York: Crossroad, 1983), 138.

[14]Mary Rose D'Angelo, "Reconstructing 'Real' Women from Gospel Literature: The Case of Mary Magdalene," in *Women & Christian Origins*, 114.

[15]Mary Rose D'Angelo, "(Re)presentations of Women in the Gospels: John and Mark," in *Women & Christian Origins*, 145-46.

[16]Mary Rose D'Angelo, "(Re)presentations of Women in the Gospel of Matthew and Luke-Acts," in *Women & Christian Origins*, 180-81, 190.

[17]Schüssler Fiorenza, *But She Said*, 210-11.

[18]Barclay M. Newman, Jr., "A Concise Greek-English Dictionary of the New Testament," 42, in Kurt Aland et al., eds., *The Greek New Testament*, 3d ed. (Stuttgart, Ger.: United Bible Societies, 1983).

[19]Walter Bauer et al., *A Greek-English Lexicon of the New Testament* (2d ed.; Chicago: University of Chicago Press, 1979), 168.

[20]Raymond E. Brown, *An Introduction to the New Testament*

The Apostolic Life

(New York: Doubleday, 1997), 657 & n.10.

[21]Romans 15:8; I Corinthians 3:5-6; Ephesians 3:7; 6:21; Colossians 1:7, 23, 25; 4:7; I Timothy 4:6.

[22]Edith A. Castelli, "Paul on Women and Gender," in *Women & Christian Origins*, 224.

[23]Schüssler Fiorenza, *In Memory of Her*, 171.

[24]Bauer et al., 718.

[25]Newman, "Dictionary," 151, in *Greek New Testament*.

[26]Romans 12:8; I Thessalonians 5:12; I Timothy 3:4-5, 12; 5:17.

[27]Romans 16:9, 21; I Corinthians 3:6-9; II Corinthians 8:23; Philippians 2:25; 4:3; Colossians 4:10-11; I Thessalonians 3:2; Philemon 1, 24.

[28]Bauer et al., 787, emphasis in original.

[29]John Chrysostom, *Homilies on Paul* 31 (*NPNF* 11:1010).

[30]Bauer et al., 380.

[31]Margaret Y. MacDonald, "Reading Real Women through the Undisputed Letters of Paul," in *Women & Christian Origins*, 209-10.

[32]I Corinthians 15:10; Galatians 4:11; Philippians 2:16; Colossians 1:29; I Timothy 4:10.

[33]I Corinthians 16:16; I Thessalonians 5:12; I Timothy 5:17.

[34]MacDonald, "Real Women," in *Women & Christian Origins*, 209.

[35]Malina, "Understanding New Testament Persons," in *Social Sciences*, 50.

[36]Schüssler Fiorenza, *But She Said*, 64.

[37]James R. Hollingshead, *The Household of Caesar and the Body of Christ: A Political Interpretation of the Letters from Paul* (Lanham, Md.: University Press of America, 1998), 126, 136.

[38]Ibid., 239, 241, 243.

[39]Ibid., 176, 187-88.

[40]Bauer et al., 442.

[41]Ehrman, *New Testament*, 368.

[42]The following start a new paragraph at verse 34: Textus Receptus, Westcott and Hort, KJV, RV, NKJV. The following begin the new paragraph in middle of verse 33: ASV, RSV, NEB, NIV, NRSV.

[43]Gordon Fee, *God's Empowering Presence: The Holy Spirit in the Letters of Paul* (Peabody, Mass.: Hendrickson, 1994), 281.

[44]Ehrman, *New Testament*, 370.

[45]Aland et al., eds., *Greek New Testament*, 611.

[46]Paul J. Achtemeier, Joel B. Green, and Marianne Meye Thompson, *Introducing the New Testament: Its Literature and Theology* (Grand Rapids: Eerdmans, 2001), 345-46.

[47]Keith Hopkins, *A World Full of Gods: The Strange Triumph of Christianity* (New York: Penguin Putnam, 1999), 214.

[48]Ross S. Kraemer, "Jewish Women and Women's Judaism(s) at the Beginning of Christianity," in *Women & Christian Origins*, 65.

[49]Lucretia B. Yaghjian, "Ancient Reading," in *Social Sciences*, 217, 220.

[50]Newman, "Dictionary," 81, *Greek New Testament*.

[51]Ibid., 28.

[52]Brown, *New Testament*, 660-61.

[53]Hippolytus, *Refutation of All Heresies* 8.12 (*ANF* 5:255-56).

[54]Paul Johnson, *A History of Christianity* (New York: Atheneum, 1977), 49.

[55]*Acts of Paul and Thecla* (*ANF* 8:1035-37).

[56]Tertullian, *On Baptism* 17 (*ANF* 3:1271-72).

[57]Francine Cardman, "Women, Ministry, and Church Order in Early Christianity," in *Women & Christian Origins*, 308, 320.

[58]Castelli, "Paul on Women and Gender," in *Women & Christian Origins*, 228-29.

[59]Karlyn Kohrs Campbell, "The Rhetoric of Women's Liberation: An Oxymoron," in *Methods of Rhetorical Criticism: A Twentieth-Century Perspective*, 3d rev. ed. (eds. Bernard Brock et al.; Detroit: Wayne State University Press, 1990), 400.

Unpublished paper written for Master's of Theology program, University of South Africa, May 27, 2003

OUTREACH

CHAPTER 34

The Paradox of the Cross (Easter)

If someone wanted to start a new religion and ensure its worldwide acceptance, what message would be most appealing to the masses? Some may think that the key to success is a message of self-esteem, positive mental attitude, and positive confession in order to obtain earthly desires. But paradoxically, the early Christian church proclaimed that true spiritual victory lies in a message of apparent defeat, namely, the death of Jesus Christ on a cross: "For the message of the cross is foolishness to those who are perishing, but to us who are being saved it is the power of God" (I Corinthians 1:18, NKJV).

In the first century, preaching about the cross was seemingly an obstacle to the acceptance of Christian beliefs. The apostle Paul wrote that some people requested a sign while others sought after wisdom, but he preached "Christ crucified," even though this message was a stumbling block to the former and foolishness to the latter (I Corinthians 1:22-23).

Some looked for a divinely anointed leader who would bring military victory and political deliverance from the

259

Roman Empire. To them it was offensive to hear that they should follow the teaching of a young man who had been executed as a common criminal by Roman authority. The preaching of the cross was thus an obstacle.

Others had great tolerance for and even interest in a variety of religious and philosophical ideas, but the message that salvation comes through a man who died, and furthermore that this man had become victorious by miraculously rising from the dead, seemed foolish in comparison. For instance, the Athenians were quite willing to listen to the novel ideas of Paul, but when he began to speak about the resurrection, most of them lost interest (Acts 17:18-33). His preaching seemed like an idle tale to those schooled in the philosophy of the day.

For everyone in the first century, the cross was an instrument of torture and execution of criminals. The mention of a cross brought to mind the sight of humiliation, the smell of blood, and the sound of agonizing cries. To people everywhere, a cross represented pain, condemnation, cruelty, and death.

Preaching about a cross in that day would be like preaching about an electric chair today. Imagine spotting a church building with an electric chair for its visual identification. Or imagine walking into a church to hear the congregation singing "The Old Rugged Hangman's Noose," "Near the Lethal Injection," or "When I Survey the Wondrous Firing Squad." It would certainly seem like a foolish way to attract visitors and make converts.

Paradoxically, Christians believe that God has chosen the foolishness of preaching, and specifically the seemingly foolish message of the cross, as the means of salvation. He has transformed the cross from an instrument of suffering, punishment, and death into an instrument of healing, deliverance, and eternal life. By the message of the cross, He likewise transforms sinners into saints, blasphemers into missionaries, and persecutors into preachers—as Paul's own life testifies.

In short, the focal point of Christianity is "Jesus Christ and Him crucified" (I Corinthians 2:2, NKJV). The good news that brings deliverance is that Jesus Christ, as God manifested in the flesh, died for our sins, was buried in a tomb, and rose again on the third day. We are to respond to this message and apply it to our lives personally by turning away from sin in repentance (death to the old life of sin and self-will), being baptized in the name of Jesus Christ (burial with Christ), and receiving the gift of the Holy Spirit (resurrection life). (See Acts 2:38.)

The cross is so powerful that it changes human hearts and transforms human lives. A host of twenty-first-century believers can testify that the message of the cross heals sick bodies and minds, delivers those bound by addictive habits and sinful behaviors, restores marriages and family relationships, and offers new beginnings, new hope, and new life.

Austin American-Statesman, August 28, 2004, under the title "Cross represents pain, salvation"

CHAPTER 35

After the Passion of the Christ (Easter)

To the surprise of the entertainment and media industries, *The Passion of the Christ* was a notable box-office success. Regardless of what you think about the movie, it drew attention to a central teaching of Christianity: Jesus Christ died to redeem us from our sins. Christianity is unique among world religions in depending upon the death of its founder. Yet there is more to Christianity's message than His suffering and death.

The New Testament proclaims that after Jesus died and was buried, He arose from the grave on the third day. To His disciples, "he shewed himself alive after his passion by many infallible proofs, being seen of them forty days, and speaking of the things pertaining to the kingdom of God" (Acts 1:3). While His death was necessary, so was His resurrection, because the resurrection turned seeming defeat into victory. By the resurrection, Jesus conquered sin and death and gave us the hope of eternal life with Him. Thus, Christianity is also unique among religions in depending on the resurrection of its founder.

But there is still more! The Bible promises that if we

believe on Jesus and obey His gospel, we can enter into the kingdom of God, which God has established in the hearts of believers. Just as Christ died and was buried, so we should identify with His death by turning away from our sins and identifying with His burial by water baptism in His name. And just as He arose to new life, so we should receive the gift of the Holy Spirit, which imparts spiritual life to us. We thereby receive God's abiding presence and obtain power to live a new life characterized by love, joy, peace, and righteousness. (See Acts 2:38; Romans 6:1-4.)

To emphasize this message, Jesus gave specific instructions to His disciples "after his passion" and just before His ascension into heaven. "He commanded them not to depart from Jerusalem, but to wait for the Promise of the Father, 'which,' He said, 'you have heard from Me; for John truly baptized with water, but you shall be baptized with the Holy Spirit not many days from now'" (Acts 1:4-5, NKJV).

The disciples obeyed this command. About 120 of them—including the twelve apostles, Mary the mother of Jesus, the four half-brothers of Jesus, and a number of women—waited in an upper room in Jerusalem, praying for the promise. On the Day of Pentecost, a Jewish religious festival, they were all filled with the Holy Spirit. (See Acts 2:1-4.)

Based on this account, Pentecostal Christians emphasize that it is important not only to believe in and contemplate Christ's passion but also to believe in His resurrection and be baptized with the Holy Spirit. We should grieve over Christ's suffering and death, and over our own sins, but we also need to obey the command and receive the promise that He gave "after his passion."

Because He died and rose again, we can obtain forgiveness of sins, deliverance from spiritual bondage, physical and emotional healing, and miraculous power to transform our lives.

Soon we will observe Good Friday and then Easter Sunday. This season reminds us that our sins caused the crucifixion of Christ, and thus it teaches us to turn away from those sins. On Easter, we will rejoice in the victory of His resurrection, which brings hope to all humans. But the story is complete when we personally receive the promise of Pentecost, which He gave us "after his passion," and enter into a new spiritual life.

Austin American-Statesman, March 20, 2004, under the title "The Bible's passion is not just a movie, but a lesson for us"

CHAPTER 36

Celebrating the Day of Pentecost

In late spring, both Jews and Christians celebrate the Day of Pentecost. For Jews, it is Shavuot—originally marking the end of the spring grain harvest in Palestine but now also commemorating the giving of the law of Moses on Mount Sinai.

For Christians, Pentecost is the birthday of the New Testament church—the day of the coming of the Holy Spirit on the disciples of Jesus, fifty days after the Passover in which Jesus died. (The name "Pentecost" means "fiftieth" in Greek.)

The story is recorded in The Acts of the Apostles, chapters 1 and 2. According to this biblical account, when Jesus ascended to heaven, He instructed His followers to wait in Jerusalem for a special promise from God. "In a few days you will be baptized [immersed] with the Holy Spirit" (Acts 1:5, NIV). He told them. "You will receive power when the Holy Spirit comes on you" (Acts 1:8, NIV). The Spirit of God would dwell in them, liberate them from sin, guide them in righteousness, and empower them for service. Soon after, on the Day of Pentecost, God's

Spirit filled all 120 waiting disciples, including the twelve apostles and Mary the mother of Jesus.

When the Holy Spirit came, the believers began to speak miraculously in languages they had never learned and did not know, as the initial sign of Spirit baptism. The apostle Peter explained to the amazed onlookers that this experience was foretold by the Hebrew prophet Joel, who proclaimed that God would pour out His Spirit on "all flesh"—men and women, young and old, and people of every walk of life. The New Testament and early post-biblical writings document that this message and experience accompanied the early Christian church as it spread around the Mediterranean world in the first and second centuries.

While many Christian groups do not expect similar miracles today, a significant number of them do, and consequently they are often called Pentecostals. "Pentecost" does not refer to a denomination but to an experience. Pentecostals hold that every believer can have a personal relationship with God characterized by His indwelling presence and miraculous power. Consequently, they pray fervently, worship joyfully, and receive physical and emotional healing, deliverance, and new spiritual life.

An important group of Pentecostals is the United Pentecostal Church International, which has thousands of congregations in 177 nations. Our fellowship believes that there is one God who has revealed himself as Father of the human race, who came in his Son Jesus Christ to save us from sin, and who manifests himself as the Holy Spirit to work in our lives. We emphasize that God is one in personality, but in addition we believe that Jesus Christ is the one true God manifested in human flesh.

We teach the importance of believing on Jesus as Savior and Lord, turning away from sin (repentance), being baptized in water in the name of Jesus Christ, being baptized with the Holy Spirit with the sign of speaking in tongues, and living a holy life by God's power. By God's grace we have seen many people overcome bad choices, addictions, abuse, prejudice, brokenness, and tragedy—making a new start, becoming whole, and enjoying abundant life. Our goal is to build strong faith, strong friendships, strong families, and strong communities.

Austin American-Statesman, May 4, 2002, under the title of "This month, we celebrate Pentecost, the birthday of the Christian church" and *South Texas Vision*, May–June 2006

CHAPTER 37

Free Indeed!
(Independence Day)

Americans are fortunate to live in the freest country in history. Although our society is far from perfect, it still affords us great economic, political, and religious liberty.

Some time ago, I was reminded of this truth on a trip to Vietnam to teach a seminar for pastors. Because the country's communist government severely curtails religious activity, we met clandestinely in a home. We ended the seminar a day early because of police surveillance in the area. A few months before, our missionary had been placed under house arrest and interrogated for four days because he helped conduct a religious meeting.

As a society, we must understand that true freedom begins with the liberty to worship God according to the dictates of conscience. When freedom of worship is curtailed, then all other freedoms—including the freedoms of speech, assembly, and the press—come under attack. Once society minimizes the belief in God, then it becomes easier to deny the reality of eternal moral law and inalienable human rights. Freedom becomes relative, and government begins to define what freedom it will allow.

Jesus pointed out that we have freedom only to the extent that we know truth. "Ye shall know the truth," He said, "and the truth shall make you free" (John 8:32). Real freedom is not based on changing human opinions but on the absolutes of God's moral order. It is not freedom to ignore truth but to understand truth and act accordingly. For instance, a person who drives off a cliff in defiance of the law of gravity is not free but ignorant, and that ignorance destroys him or her. In this situation, freedom is the ability to know the truth about the law of gravity and to avoid the danger posed by the cliff.

Freedom in the highest sense, then, is the knowledge of right from wrong coupled with the ability to choose right. It means recognizing the benefits of right values and the devastating consequences of wrong values, and having the courage and strength to guide our lives, families, and communities according to the former. Spiritual freedom consists of deliverance from destructive patterns of thought and behavior and fulfillment of God's will for our lives.

Governments can neither bestow nor take away this freedom, for it must come from God. Jesus said, "If the Son therefore shall make you free, ye shall be free indeed" (John 8:36). The believers in Vietnam do not enjoy religious or political freedom, but they do have spiritual freedom, and as such they are free indeed!

Spiritual freedom is the work of the living Lord in the believer's life by the power of His Spirit. "Now the Lord is that Spirit: and where the Spirit of the Lord is, there is liberty" (II Corinthians 3:17). Regardless of political and economic circumstances, we can enjoy the highest freedom when we are filled with God's Spirit and live by His liberating power every day.

Northwest Austin Life and Times, July 17, 1998, under the title "True freedom begins with the liberty to worship"; *Forward*, April-June 1999; *New Life News*, Austin, Texas, Fall 2003; *Austin American-Statesman*, August 24, 2002, under the title "First, know the truth, then act on it"

CHAPTER 38

The Significance of a Name
(Christmas)

Parents today usually choose a name for their child because they like its sound or perhaps because they wish to honor someone who bears that name. Often they do not know the original meaning of the name they have chosen.

In ancient times, however, a name was usually chosen for its meaning. The Bible records many instances in which a child's name related to the circumstances surrounding the child's birth or to the aspirations of the parents for their child. A person's name was regarded as the essence and expression of his or her personality.

In a similar manner, God used names and titles to reveal Himself. In the Bible, God's name signifies His self-revelation, particularly His character, power, authority, and manifested presence.

According to the New Testament, Jesus was named by an angel before He was ever born. The name "Jesus" incorporates the Hebrew name for God—Yahweh (Jehovah)—and it means "Yahweh-savior" or "Yahweh is salvation." The name "Yahweh," in turn, is probably derived from the verb "to be," meaning "He is" or "He will be," and thus it refers to God as the self-existing, eternal, and all-powerful one.

Although others have borne the name Jesus, Jesus Christ of Nazareth is the only one who actually personifies that name in the fullest sense. The noted Protestant theologian Karl Barth wrote, "God himself, in his deep mercy and its great power, has taken it upon himself to exist also in human being and essence in his Son. . . . God himself has assumed and made his own our human nature and kind in his Son, just because God himself came into this world in his Son. . . . He gives himself to be the humanly acting and suffering person [on the cross]."

We confess that Jesus is the eternal, almighty God who became incarnate in order to be the savior of humanity. As a human He is known as the Son of God, or God manifested in the flesh. In the words of Isaiah, He is Immanuel, or "God with us."

Praying in the name of Jesus expresses faith in His divine character (love, compassion, and desire to help), power (ability to help), authority (right to help), and presence (immediate attention and availability to help). For this reason, the apostles in the New Testament prayed for the sick to be healed in the name of Jesus, cast out demons in the name of Jesus, and baptized all believers with the invocation of the name of Jesus.

We believe that God still answers when believers pray in the name of Jesus today. Thus, we expect to receive forgiveness, healing, deliverance, and the power of the Holy Spirit when we pray with faith in the name of Jesus. Not only is this name invoked upon us during the initial act of water baptism, but it remains with us to give power and authority that comes from the presence of Jesus Christ, who abides and actively works in our daily lives.

Austin American-Statesman, December 13, 2003; *New Life News*, Austin, Texas, Summer 2005

CHAPTER 39

Faith That Transforms

Everyone has faith in something, for without faith it is impossible to survive. Whether we trust in ourselves, others, money, tradition, philosophy, or God, we all believe in something.

Christianity teaches that ultimately we must trust in God. While we need to take responsibility for our actions, we cannot, by our ability and performance, ensure our spiritual well-being or earn eternal life. Instead, we are saved by grace—the free gift of God—and we receive this gift through faith—by following His plan instead of our own ideas, by depending on God's work in our lives instead of our own goodness.

Pentecostal Christians emphasize that faith is not merely accepting a set of beliefs, but it is an experience with God and a new way of life. In the fullest sense, faith means reliance and commitment, and it requires obedience to what we believe. If someone runs into the workplace yelling, "The building is on fire!" the response of faith is not merely a grin, a nod, and verbal acceptance. Rather, if we believe the warning, we will immediately act upon it. Dietrich Bonhoeffer, a German theologian executed by the Nazis, said, "Only he who is obedient believes."

When Jesus called some Galilean fishermen to be His disciples, He said, "Follow me." They did not become disciples merely by believing Him to be the Messiah, Lord, and Savior, or by verbally confessing Him as such. They became His disciples only when they obeyed His instructions, cast aside their nets, and began to follow Him. Faith is only real in the act of obedience.

Christianity is more than mental acknowledgment, verbal profession, or even performance of religious duties. If we truly have faith in Jesus Christ, we will obey His gospel, and our lives will be transformed by His Spirit. Thus Pentecostals emphasize the importance of repentance (a decision to turn away from sin), baptism in the name of Jesus Christ, and receiving the gift of the Holy Spirit. (See Acts 2:38.) Through the power of God, then, we are able to work for the transformation of human lives and human society.

Years ago, tightrope walkers used to demonstrate their talents by walking on a wire stretched over Niagara Falls. Crowds would gather to see this incredibly dangerous feat. Once, a performer promised to push a wheelbarrow across the wire. First, however, he wanted assurance from the audience that they believed he could do it. Eagerly, the crowd roared its approval several times.

Finally, the performer pointed to one of his most vocal supporters and said, "Jump in! I'll wheel you across." Neither this man nor anyone else would accept the offer. They had "faith" in the sense of opinion or agreement, but they were not willing to commit their lives to what they professed.

What kind of faith do we have? What kind of faith does God expect?

Northwest Austin Life & Times, August 14, 1998; *Forward*, April-June 1999; *New Life Young Families News*, 2002; *Austin American-Statesman*, May 10, 2003, under the title "Faith in God starts with acts of obedience, not just a belief in ideals"

CHAPTER 40

Forgiveness

If we are honest, we will admit that the Bible is not only generally correct but also specifically accurate in our case when it says, "All have sinned, and come short of the glory of God" (Romans 3:23). Because of our sin, we deserve eternal death, but God has extended grace and mercy to us so that we can enjoy the blessings of forgiveness and eternal life! "For the wages of sin is death; but the gift of God is eternal life through Jesus Christ our Lord" (Romans 6:23).

The Bible also teaches that genuine repentance is a prerequisite to receive forgiveness. "He who covers his sins will not prosper, but whoever confesses and forsakes them will have mercy" (Proverbs 28:13, NKJV).

If we persist in sinful behavior, we will eventually reap what we sow (Galatians 6:7). By the grace of God, we have an alternative: we can impose consequences on ourselves now by confessing our sins to God and by seeking help to change our ways. If we sin against others, we need to make things right with them. Doing so can be painful and embarrassing, but it is the path of mercy and forgiveness.

At the same time, we must be willing to forgive others who have sinned but who want to change their ways. Even before they make things right, we must pray for a heart of forgiveness and a willingness to be merciful. Jesus taught that God will continue to forgive us as long as we are willing to extend forgiveness to others (Matthew 6:14-15).

If we merely try to evade all consequences of sin by covering up wrongdoing and yet expecting forgiveness anyway, we only deceive ourselves. We do not deal with the problems in our lives or obtain the help we need, and we set a trap for ourselves in the future.

Each of us must take personal responsibility for our actions. If we have done wrong, we must admit it to ourselves and to God. Then we must admit it to those to whom we are accountable, we must seek to correct our ways, and we must ask forgiveness.

In this way, forgiveness becomes not a trap in our future but a deliverance from our past. Through repentance and forgiveness, we are liberated from our past so that we can enjoy a blessed, productive present and future.

Northwest Austin Life & Times, September 18, 1998, under the title "Forgiveness without repentance doesn't work"; *New Life News*, Summer 2003; *Forward*, April-June 1999

CHAPTER 41

Humanity's Relationship with God

One of the most striking characteristics of the human race is that all cultures incorporate a belief in the supernatural and the divine. Throughout human history the overwhelming majority of people have believed in the existence of God. Every society has basic concepts of morality, of ethical right and wrong, and of spirituality that transcend practical and selfish considerations.

The history of religion is a record of humanity's age-old quest to know God and to understand His will. How can we determine whether this quest is well-founded, and if it is, which way is right?

Humanity's Search for God

In the first part of the twentieth century, anthropologists commonly believed that religion had evolved from the primitive to the profound. According to this theory, early humans observed awesome phenomena in nature that they could not explain or control—such as powerful animals, mountains, rivers, fire, thunder, lightning—and attributed supernatural characteristics to them. Polytheism, the belief in many gods, was born. Prayer, worship, ritual, and magic came into being as attempts to appease these often destructive forces and to enlist their aid. As society grew more complex and sophisticated, so did religion. A hierarchy of gods developed, and finally a supreme God emerged. The focus of religion then shifted from magic to morality.

The problem with this theory is that it is historically and empirically false. In their study of preliterary cultures, anthropologists and sociologists have found that even the most primitive people have a belief in God. They have been unable to find a pre-God stage in any culture. More-over, the notion of a creator god or a high god—one who rules over all other forces or gods—is there from the out-set. In some cases, he is identified as the only true God.

Unfortunately, most preliterary societies developed the idea that the supreme God was too lofty for mere mortals to approach, and so they turned to lesser gods as mediators and benefactors. The result was a proliferation of religions in humanity's search for divine truth.

Does God Really Exist?

Is the universal belief in God valid? Ultimately, know-ing God is a matter of faith, but it is a reasonable faith, much more reasonable than the alternative.

Our very existence testifies to the reality of the Cre-ator. There can be only one of three explanations for the existence of the universe: (1) it has always existed (eter-nal universe); (2) it came into existence by its own power (self-creating universe), or (3) God created it. Accepting any of these requires a faith that transcends scientific proof. It is more plausible to believe in an intelligent, eternal, all-powerful Creator than in the eternity or self-creative ability of nonrational matter.

The orderliness and design of the universe require the existence of a Designer. The incredible complexity of even the simplest forms of life shows that life did not begin by accident or blind chance. Our moral nature reveals that we are more than intelligent animals; we were created in the image of a rational, spiritual, moral Being. Every human child develops a conscience, and every human society has a sense of morality. How could the finite human mind even conceive of an infinite, all-powerful, all-knowing, perfect God, and why would humans have universally embraced that concept, unless God had imparted it?

How Can We Know God?

Many religions have arisen as a consequence of the universal, ancient belief in God, and they offer various human theories about God. They stand as testimony to humanity's search for God. If we acknowledge that the all-powerful, all-knowing God created us for His purpose, however, it would seem more important to discover what He has revealed about Himself than to study what various people have surmised about Him.

We would expect the Creator to communicate with His creation. Since God created us as rational beings and since He loves us enough to provide for us, surely He wishes to communicate with us and thereby fulfill His purpose for creation. All intelligent beings seek to communicate, and the Supreme Intelligence is no exception.

One means of communication is the spoken word, and numerous individuals have stated that God spoke to them. Some have presented themselves as prophets—people ordained to speak on God's behalf. Given the flaws of human nature, however, we would expect that at least some of these reputed prophets would actually be false prophets, whether misguided or dishonest.

How can we test such claims and discern between true and false prophets? Several questions can help us in this determination. Were the people who claimed to be prophets known to be honest, credible, and moral? Did their lives support their message? Did they advocate worship of the one true God, or did they introduce the worship of false gods? Did their message agree with prior revelation from God? Did the people of God in their day recognize them as prophets? Did they seek to build a personal following, or did they seek only to advance the kingdom of God? Did their predictions come to pass? Has their message stood the test of time?

Ultimately, it is difficult to judge a message until it has been expressed in a permanent form. In fact, we would expect God to record His message in writing, the historic medium best suited for precision, preservation, and propagation.

The following evidence convincingly demonstrates that the Bible is the unique written Word of God to humanity: (1) its unique claims, (2) self-vindicating authority, (3) testimony of the apostles and prophets, (4) integrity of Jesus Christ, who endorsed the Old Testament and commissioned the writers of the New, (5) nature and quality of its content, (6) moral superiority, (7) unity, despite more than forty writers over 1,600 years, (8) lack of a credible alternative, (9) agreement with history, archaeology, and science, (10) indestructibility, (11) universality, (12) influence on society, (13) witness of the Holy Spirit, (14) lack of an alternative explanation of its origin, (15) fulfilled promises and miracles, (16) fulfilled prophecies, and (17) life-changing power. (For further discussion, see David K. Bernard, *God's Infallible Word*.)

We would certainly expect God's Word to identify itself as such, and the Bible repeatedly claims throughout to be the Word of God. The world's most moral book, the Bible, would not proclaim what would be the world's biggest lie. The world's noblest and wisest person, Jesus, would not perpetrate what would be the world's greatest hoax.

Events in modern times—such as the reestablishment of Israel as a nation after 1,800 years of dispersion—have dramatically fulfilled biblical prophecies that skeptics long dismissed. Multitudes in our day have received in their own lives the miraculous promises of the Bible, including deliverance from sinful habits and lifestyles by the power of the Holy Spirit.

Once we acknowledge the Bible as God's Word, we can use it to evaluate other prophetic claims. For example, it brands as false any prophet who leads people to believe in more than one eternal God of the universe (Deuteronomy 6:4; 13:1-3; Isaiah 43:10; 44:6, 8).

The Bible contains all the instruction we need to be saved and to live a godly life (II Timothy 3:15-17). Its message is sufficient and complete (II Peter 1:3). Any message that adds to or takes away from the Bible is false (Revelation 22:18-19). This is so whether the new message comes from a human or an angel, from an apostle or a prophet. The apostle Paul declared of the gospel that the early church preached: "Even if we, or an angel from heaven, preach any other gospel to you than what we have preached to you, let him be accursed. As we have said before, so now I say again, if anyone preaches any other gospel to you than what you have received, let him be accursed" (Galatians 1:8-9, NKJV).

Any prophetic message outside the Bible, then, is not necessary for us and could be dangerous. If it is of spiritual importance and truth, then it is already contained in the Bible. If it purports to teach needed spiritual truth not already revealed in the Bible, then it is false.

How Can We Be Saved?

The Bible proclaims that every human being has sinned (Romans 3:23), and this declaration corresponds to our own observation and experience. Moreover, the Bible teaches us that God is holy and as such cannot have fellowship with sin. The consequence of our sin is death—separation from God (Romans 6:23). Since all have sinned, all are under the sentence of eternal death.

But God has provided a way of salvation for us through Jesus Christ, the Son of God. Jesus was actually God manifested in the flesh (John 20:28; I Timothy 3:16). He died on the cross for our sins, taking our penalty upon Himself (Matthew 20:28; Romans 3:24-25). The gospel, or good news, is that Jesus died for our sins, was buried in a tomb, and rose again on the third day (I Corinthians 15:1-4). By believing on Him and obeying His gospel, we can know God, have fellowship with Him, and inherit eternal life.

The Bible states emphatically that salvation is a free gift of God that we cannot earn, merit, purchase, or deserve: "For by grace you have been saved through faith, and that not of yourselves; it is the gift of God, not of works, lest anyone should boast" (Ephesians 2:8-9, NKJV).

Human religions typically prescribe methods by which we are to attract God's attention, earn His favor, and qualify ourselves for spiritual advancement. These efforts are doomed to failure, however, because none of us can ever do anything to deserve salvation. Rather, we must accept the free offer of salvation that God has provided in Jesus.

The Bible rebukes those who seek to make themselves righteous by their own works, those who trust in their own efforts for divine approval and spiritual status. "A man is justified by faith apart from the deeds of the law" (Romans 3:28, NKJV). "But that no one is justified by the law in the sight of God is evident, for 'the just shall live by faith'" (Galatians 3:11, NKJV). "Not by works of righteousness which we have done, but according to His mercy He saved us" (Titus 3:5, NKJV).

Salvation comes through faith in Jesus Christ—trusting in His work instead of our own, boasting of His merits instead of ours. By relying upon what Christ has done for us and committing our lives to Him, we can enjoy God's grace—His unmerited favor and saving power. Instead of living in constant fear and uncertainty about our worthiness, we can have spiritual peace and assurance, knowing that we are justified—counted as righteous—by faith in Jesus.

Of course, saving faith is more than mental acknowledgment or verbal profession. It is a firm commitment, an active reliance that comes alive when we obey the gospel. Only those who believe are obedient, and only those who are obedient believe.

The Bible speaks of "obedience to the faith" (Romans 1:5; 16:26), showing that we cannot separate faith from obedience. If we believe on Jesus we will believe His Word, and if we believe His Word we will follow it. Faith in the gospel of Jesus Christ includes obeying that gospel in our own lives. We are saved by obeying Christ, by obeying His teaching (doctrine) (Romans 6:17; Hebrews 5:9). Those who refuse to obey the gospel of Jesus Christ will not be saved (II Thessalonians 1:8-9; I Peter 4:17).

The obedience of faith does not mean that we earn salvation. God performs the work of salvation in us, doing for us what we cannot do for ourselves: forgiving our sins, counting us as righteous in His sight, filling us with His Spirit, enabling us to live a holy life. But we must open our hearts to His saving work, applying the gospel personally.

How do we exercise saving faith and experience God's saving grace in our lives? How do we personally respond to and apply the gospel of Jesus Christ? The apostle Peter, with the support of the rest of the apostles, answered this question on the birthday of the Christian church: "Repent, and let every one of you be baptized in the name of Jesus Christ for the remission of sins; and you shall receive the gift of the Holy Spirit" (Acts 2:38, NKJV).

Repentance means a turn from sin to God. It is a death to self-will and the sinful way of life, and as such, it identifies us with Christ's death on the cross. Baptism by immersion in water, having the name of Jesus called over us, identifies us with His burial (Romans 6:3-4). And when we receive the Holy Spirit, we receive the resurrection life of the Lord (Romans 8:2, 10). When we are filled with the Spirit, we will miraculously speak in a language we never learned as the initial sign of this experience (Acts 2:4).

When we turn to the Lord in faith according to the instructions of Acts 2:38, we can enjoy the fullness of salvation that God has provided for us. Our quest for divine truth and fellowship will be fulfilled.

This experience is for everyone today. As Peter proclaimed in Acts 2:39 (NKJV), "The promise is to you and to your children, and to all who are afar off, as many as the Lord our God will call."

Special UPCI newsletter distributed at General Conference, Salt Lake City, October 1992; *Pentecostal Herald*, November 1992, under the title "The Quest for Divine Truth"

CHAPTER 42

The Way of Salvation

Faith and Repentance

Life's greatest challenges are sin and death. Only the Bible tells us the root problem: All have sinned and broken fellowship with the one, holy God, who is the only source of life. That is the bad news.

The good news is, God loved us so much that He came into this world as Jesus Christ, the Son of God, to restore fellowship. As a sinless human, Jesus died in our place and rose again, winning victory over sin and death. He now offers salvation as God's gift.

How can we receive this gift? The Bible tells us to believe on Jesus. Saving faith means more than agreement or confession; it involves trusting and obeying Jesus as Lord. For instance, if someone shouts, "The building is on fire!" the occupants will be delivered only if they run outside. They are saved as they respond in obedient faith.

In Acts 2:38, the twelve apostles proclaimed the message of salvation: Repent, be baptized in the name of Jesus Christ, and receive the gift of God's Holy Spirit.

The first response of faith is repentance, which

means turning from sin to God—confessing our sins to Him and deciding to forsake them. This step prepares us for baptism of water and Spirit, and this complete experience brings new life.

Water Baptism

The first step of faith in God is repentance. It means to confess sins to God and to turn from sin and self-will. Thus, repentance is a death to the old life.

After death comes burial. The apostle Paul wrote in Romans 6 that we are buried with Jesus Christ in water baptism. On the birthday of the Christian church, in Acts 2, the apostles proclaimed, "Repent, and be baptized every one of you in the name of Jesus Christ for the remission of sins . . . "

At repentance and water baptism, God forgives our sins, wipes our record clean, and prepares our hearts to receive His Spirit. Thus baptism is part of salvation—not by our works but by the work of God in us.

In the first-century church, people were baptized as soon as they believed on Jesus and repented, even in the middle of the night or the middle of the wilderness. They were always immersed in water and with the invocation of the name of Jesus, to signify burial with Him. It is important to call His name, because Jesus is the only name given for our salvation. When we are baptized in Jesus' name, we exercise faith in Jesus Christ as our Savior, the One who takes away our sin.

The Gift of the Holy Spirit

Just before Jesus ascended to heaven, He commanded His followers to wait until they were baptized with the Holy Spirit. To be baptized means to be plunged or immersed. Thus, He promised an overwhelming experience of being filled, empowered, and transformed by the presence of the one true God. Believers would receive the resurrection life of Christ to abide in them.

About 120 disciples received this promise on the birthday of the Christian church in Acts 2. As the initial sign, they began to speak miraculously in languages they had never learned, by the power of the Spirit.

This wonderful experience fulfilled the words of the prophet Joel that God would pour out His Spirit on all flesh. As the church expanded throughout the first century, people from all backgrounds received the Holy Spirit with the sign of speaking in tongues.

God wants everyone to enter into this new life. The apostle Peter, with the support of the other church leaders, proclaimed for all who would believe and repent: "You shall receive the gift of the Holy Spirit. For the promise is to you and to your children, and to all who are afar off, as many as the Lord our God will call" (Acts 2:38, NKJV).

Summary and Conclusion

The Bible proclaims that every human being has sinned, and this declaration corresponds to our own observation and experience. Moreover, the Bible teaches that God is holy and cannot have fellowship with sin. The consequence of our sin is death—separation from God. Since all have sinned, all are under the sentence of eternal death.

God has provided a way of salvation for us through Jesus Christ, the Son of God. "For God so loved the world that He gave His only begotten Son, that whoever believes in Him should not perish but have everlasting life" (John 3:16, NKJV).

Jesus was actually God manifested in the flesh. He lived a sinless life, and thus He was the only person who never deserved to die. Nevertheless, He died on the cross for us, taking our penalty upon Himself. The gospel, or good news, is that Jesus died for our sins, was buried in a tomb, and rose again on the third day. By believing on Him and obeying His gospel, we can have fellowship with God and inherit eternal life.

The Bible states emphatically that salvation is a free gift of God that we cannot earn, merit, purchase, or deserve. "For by grace you have been saved through faith, and that not of yourselves; it is the gift of God, not of works, lest anyone should boast" (Ephesians 2:8, NKJV).

How do we exercise saving faith and experience God's saving grace in our lives? How do we personally respond to and apply the gospel of Jesus Christ?

The apostle Peter, with the support of the rest of the apostles, answered this question on the birthday of the Christian church, as recorded in the Book of Acts, chapter 2, verse 38. He instructed everyone to repent, be baptized in the name of Jesus Christ, and receive the gift of the Holy Spirit. Through repentance, which is a turn away from sin and a death to sin, we are crucified with Christ. Through water baptism we are buried with Christ. By receiving the gift of the Holy Spirit, we share in Christ's resurrection.

While He was on earth, Jesus promised that He would prepare an eternal home for His church and then return one day to bring them to that place to live with Him forever. After His resurrection from the dead, Jesus met with

His disciples over a period of forty days and then ascended to heaven. After His ascension, two angels announced that Jesus would return to earth in the same way that He had left.

According to Bible prophecy, we are living in the last days. Just as He promised, Jesus Christ is coming back to earth soon to take His church to the eternal city that He has prepared. Now is the time to get ready for His coming. On the last page of the Bible, we find this invitation: "And the Spirit and the bride say, 'Come!' And let him who hears say, 'Come!' And let him who thirsts come. Whoever desires, let him take the water of life freely (Revelation 22:17, NKJV)."

Unpublished script for evangelistic audio CD. Biblical quotations are from the KJV and NKJV.

SCIENCE
and
SCRIPTURE

CHAPTER 43

Science and the Existence of God
Part 1

By faith, we accept the existence of God. We will never be able to convince skeptics of God's existence simply by scientific formulas or experiments, because there is no substitute for faith. "But without faith it is impossible to please him: for he that cometh to God must believe that he is, and that he is a rewarder of them that diligently seek him" (Hebrews 11:6).

Nevertheless, our faith in God is not a blind or foolish faith but a reasonable faith. There are compelling reasons why we should believe in the existence of God. Our society places great value on scientific information, and many people are hindered from believing in God because of the arguments of atheistic scientists. Therefore, we can enhance receptivity of our message by a discussion of scientific evidence.

According to the Bible, the created universe bears witness to God's existence and glory. "The heavens declare the glory of God; and the firmament sheweth his handiwork. Day unto day uttereth speech, and night unto night sheweth knowledge. There is no speech nor language, where their voice is not heard. Their line is gone out through all the earth, and their words to the end of the world" (Psalm 19:1-4).

The evidence from creation is so strong that people who deny God's identity and character are without excuse: "Since the creation of the world His invisible attributes are clearly seen, being understood by the things that are made, even His eternal power and Godhead, so that they are without excuse" (Romans 1:20, NKJV).

A study of science and Scripture often leads to debates over the age of the earth and over the theory of evolution. While these discussions are important, they are secondary to the question of origins. The ultimate question that science has tried to consider but cannot answer is: How and why does the universe exist? There are three possible explanations: (1) God created the universe. (2) The universe came into existence on its own. (3) The universe has always existed. If someone were to posit that an outside force, law, or physical state other than God brought the universe into existence, then we can simply push the question one step further: What is the origin of this force, law, or physical state? Then we are back to the three possible answers.

We should note that science cannot prove the validity of any of these answers. They can only be accepted by faith. Therefore, ultimately everyone, including scientists, can only accept an explanation of the origin of the universe by faith. One must believe in (1) an eternal God who created the universe, or (2) a universe that created itself out of nothing, or (3) an eternal universe. Each answer goes beyond all possible scientific evidence, for science cannot examine anything outside our universe or speak definitively about eternity. Each answer exceeds complete human comprehension, for we cannot fathom concepts such as eternity, omnipotence, and creation out of nothing. But we can say that faith in an eternal, creative God is at least as rational as faith in a self-creating universe or an eternal universe.

A branch of science called cosmology has arisen in an attempt to find out more about the origin and existence of the universe. Let us briefly consider what cosmology can tell us.

An Eternal Universe?

If the universe is infinitely old, then it must essentially be static. If it were eternally contracting, it would have already reached a point of complete collapse. If it were eternally expanding, it would have already reached a point of complete dissipation.

If the universe is infinitely old and static, then it must be infinitely large, as Isaac Newton showed. The reason is that in a finite but eternal universe, gravity would eventually cause everything to collapse into a central sphere. Only an infinite number of stars could evenly counterbalance the pull of gravity on each of them.

However, as Johannes Kepler and Heinrich Olbers pointed out, if the universe were infinite, then the night sky would not be dark but bright. The reason is that in an infinite universe, stars would exist at every position in the sky and light from each of them would eventually reach the earth. The dilemma of the dark night sky is known as Olbers's paradox.

Moreover, by the laws of modern physics, no star could keep burning forever. An eternal, static universe would contradict the second law of thermodynamics, which states that entropy (unusable energy, disorder) increases over time. Heat flows spontaneously from hot to cold bodies, but not vice versa, so that the universe is gradually sliding toward thermodynamic equilibrium, or heat death, where all temperatures even out.

To avoid this problem, an eternal universe would have to be eternally creating new matter/energy out of nothing and would have to look essentially the same throughout space and time. This would contradict not only the second law of thermodynamics but also the first law of thermodynamics, which says that matter/energy is neither being created nor destroyed. As we will discuss, twentieth-century discoveries have falsified the theory of an eternally self-creating universe.

A few scientists have posited an eternally oscillating universe—one that follows an endless cycle of expansion, contraction, and expansion. However, this theory would require (a) a sufficient mass in the universe so that gravity would eventually overcome the expansion and cause the contraction, and (b) an enormous repulsive force, far greater than the total motion of the universe, that would counteract the law of gravity and propel the universe outward again after its contraction. Scientists have calculated that the universe does not have enough mass to overcome expansion and furthermore have discovered no repulsive force that could make the universe bounce outward again. Additionally, the second law of thermodynamics means that less energy would be available each time the universe bounced. The successive bounces would become farther and farther apart. Extrapolating backward in time, the bounces would have been closer and closer together until they had a beginning—hence, no eternal universe.

The Big Bang

One of the equations in Einstein's general theory of relativity indicates that the universe is expanding. At first, Einstein was so startled by this contradiction of the prevailing notion of a static universe that he added a "cosmological constant" to the equation to cancel out the predicted expansion, even though this constant did not represent any observed physical phenomenon. The careful astronomical measurements of Edwin Hubble in the early twentieth century demonstrated that the universe is expanding in all directions, just as Einstein's original equation had predicted. Consequently, Einstein eliminated the cosmological constant, calling it his "greatest blunder."

Hubble made use of the Doppler effect, in which sound waves from an approaching object increase in perceived frequency (i.e., decrease in wavelength), while waves from a receding object decrease in perceived frequency (i.e., increase in wavelength). As an illustration, suppose someone throws to you one ball per second. If the thrower walks toward you, the balls will come faster because they have less distance to travel, but if the thrower walks away from you, the balls will be spaced farther apart. This effect explains why an ambulance siren sounds higher in pitch as it approaches and lower as it recedes. Hubble showed that the greater the distance of an astronomical object such as a galaxy, the more its color shifted toward the red end of the light spectrum. Red has the longest wavelength of visible light, so redshift is evidence that astronomical objects are moving away from us and therefore that the universe is expanding.

If the universe is expanding, then we can extrapolate backward in time to a point where the universe had a beginning. This insight led to the big bang theory, which states that the universe began with a powerful explosion that created matter/energy and space-time. (According to Einstein's theory of relativity, matter and energy are equivalent, and space and time form a continuum of four dimensions.)

If the big bang occurred, there should still be cosmic background radiation left over from the creation of the universe. In 1964, researchers Arno Penzias and Robert Wilson detected persistent microwave radiation coming from all directions of the sky at the temperature equivalent of about 3 degrees Kelvin (3 degrees above absolute zero, the theoretical point at which there would be no energy, no motion of particles). After careful analysis, scientists concluded that they had discovered the predicted cosmic background radiation, thus verifying the expansion of the universe and repudiating the idea of a static universe.

The universe is not completely uniform; it has clumps of matter called galaxies separated by vast expanses of almost empty space. This fact led scientists to conclude that there must have been fluctuations early in the expansion of the universe that caused wrinkles in space-time. Therefore, it must be possible to detect minute variations in the cosmic background radiation. In 1992, George Smoot and the COBE (cosmic background explorer) team discovered such wrinkles in the cosmic background radiation, thereby supporting the big bang theory. Stephen Hawking somewhat hyperbolically called this "the scientific discovery of the century, if not all time," because it solidified the foundation of modern cosmology.

Conclusion

Our faith in God does not rest upon scientific theories and discoveries, but it is intriguing that the current research in cosmology dramatically supports the biblical account of creation. The idea of an eternal universe—whether static or oscillating—has been discredited. In a future article we will discuss scientific evidence against the idea that our universe could have spontaneously and randomly exploded into existence on its own without an intelligent Creator.

The bottom line is that belief in the existence of God as the Creator of the universe is the most reasonable option of all. We do not have to accept all the theories of scientists in order to arrive at this conclusion, and we recognize that many of them still fail to acknowledge the existence of a personal Creator. Nevertheless, it is interesting that many use religious language to describe the wonder of creation.

George Smoot wrote, "There is no doubt that a parallel exists between the big bang as an event and the Christian notion of creation from nothing," and he explained the significance of his discovery by saying, "If you're religious, it's like seeing God." Astrophysicist Robert Jastrow, an agnostic, somewhat ruefully described the scientist's quest to understand cosmology: "He has scaled the mountains of ignorance; he is about to conquer the highest peak; as he pulls himself over the final rock, he is greeted by a band of theologians who have been sitting there for centuries."

Sources

Davies, Paul. *The Mind of God*. New York: Touchstone, 1992.

Einstein, Albert. *The Meaning of Relativity*, 5th ed. New York: MJF, 1956.

Jastrow, Robert. *God and the Astronomers*, 2d ed. New York: Norton, 1992.

Penrose, Roger. *The Emperor's New Mind*. New York: Oxford University Press, 1989.

Rees, Martin. *Just Six Numbers*. New York: Basic, 2000.

Ross, Hugh. *The Creator and the Cosmos*, 3d ed. Colorado Springs: NavPress, 2001.

Smoot, George, and Keay Davidson. *Wrinkles in Time*. New York: Avon, 1993.

Strobel, Lee. *The Case for a Creator*. Grand Rapids: Zondervan, 2004. (Best one-volume treatment for a general audience.)

Forward, January-February 2006

CHAPTER 44

Science and the Existence of God
Part 2

We can only accept the existence of God by faith, but it is a reasonable faith. There are three possible answers to the question of how and why the universe came into existence: (1) An eternal God created the universe. (2) The universe created itself from nothing. (3) The universe is eternal. Science cannot prove any one of these propositions; they can only be accepted by faith.

A previous article discussed scientific evidence that discounts the idea of an eternal universe. In 1970, Stephen Hawking and Roger Penrose proved mathematically that if Einstein's general theory of relativity is true, then the universe must have a beginning in time (Hawking, p. 50).

A Self-Creating Universe?

Is it reasonable to believe that the universe came into existence by its own power or without any preexisting cause? This idea violates the first law of thermodynamics, which states that in an isolated system mass/energy is neither created nor destroyed.

311

Quantum theory, which describes physics at the atomic level, does allow for some apparent, miniscule violations of this law. According to the Heisenberg uncertainty principle, it is impossible to know both the position and momentum of a subatomic particle at the same time. We can only describe the location and movement of a particle by a probability distribution.

This principle allows for the possibility of quantum fluctuations, or temporary changes in energy at a point in space. It may be that a pair of "virtual particles" can temporarily appear in a vacuum and then quickly combine to annihilate one another. Some scientists propose that the big bang occurred when pairs of virtual particles appeared in a vacuum, but somehow a particle escaped annihilation and became the seed of our universe.

This concept does not answer the question of origins, however. Even if virtual particles arise temporarily, they do not come into existence out of absolutely nothing. Instead, their existence is based on the prior existence of physical laws and energy. Quantum theory considers that background energy is present even in a vacuum, and this energy field is the source of quantum fluctuations. But if the universe came into existence out of nothing, there was no preexisting energy.

A Fine-Tuned Universe

Scientists of all philosophical and religious beliefs have discovered to their amazement that the physical laws and initial conditions of the universe are fine-tuned for the existence of human life. If the fundamental laws and constants that determine physics were altered by minute amounts, human life could not exist.

Martin Rees, an astronomer and professor at Cambridge University, described six fundamental constants in physics that must fall within an extremely narrow range in order for our universe to exist. For example, the number that measures how firmly atomic nuclei bind together is 0.007. If it were 0.006, protons would not bond to neutrons in the nucleus of an atom, and the universe would have no chemical element but hydrogen (because its nucleus consists only of one proton). If the binding force were 0.008, then two protons would bind together directly without a neutron, thus prohibiting the existence of hydrogen. Without hydrogen, there would be no water and no fuel for the sun. In short, this number must fall between 0.006 and 0.008 in order for there to be a universe capable of sustaining human life.

Stephen Hawking, probably the most famous physicist alive today, has summarized the evidence: "The laws of science, as we know them at present, contain many fundamental numbers, like the size of the electric charge of the electron and the ratio of the masses of the proton and the electron. . . . The remarkable fact is that the values of these numbers seem to have been very finely adjusted to make possible the development of life. . . . It seems clear that there are relatively few ranges of values for the numbers that would allow the development of any form of intelligent life. . . . One can take this either as evidence of a divine purpose in Creation and the choice of the laws of science or as support for the strong anthropic principle [discussed below]" (p. 125).

Roger Penrose, a colleague and former teacher of Hawking, analyzed the initial conditions that had to be present at the big bang in order for our universe to develop as it has: "In order to produce a universe resembling the one in which we live, the Creator would have to aim for an absurdly tiny volume of the phase space of possible universes, . . . one part in 10 [to the power of] 10^{123}. This is an extraordinary figure. One could not possibly even write the number down in full: . . . it would be '1' followed by 10^{123} successive '0's [and 10^{123} is one followed by 123 zeros]! Even if we were to write a '0' on each separate proton and on each separate neutron in the entire universe—and we could throw in all the other particles as well for good measure—we should fall far short of writing down the figure needed" (pp. 343-44).

Physicist Richard Morris made a similar calculation: "It appears, therefore, that we exist in a very improbable kind of universe, one that was fine-tuned to an accuracy of one part in 10^{15} at a time of one second after the big bang. In fact, this fine-tuning was even greater at earlier times. At some point, when the universe was only a fraction of a second old, it would have been not one part in 10^{15}, but one part in 10^{50}. If this fine-tuning had not taken place, we would not exist. . . . Scientists distrust coincidences. When they find that a number is that close to a critical value, they are generally unwilling to believe that this could have happened by chance. They are not satisfied until they find a reason for why the fine-tuning should be that exact" (pp. 54-55).

Hugh Ross, an astronomer formerly with the California Institute of Technology, identified 128 parameters necessary for the existence of life on a planet. He then estimated the probability for the occurrence of all 128 parameters as approximately one part in 10^{166} and the maximum possible number of planets in the universe as

10^{22}. He concluded, "Thus, less than 1 chance in 10^{144} (trillion trillion trillion trillion trillion trillion trillion trillion trillion trillion trillion trillion) exists that even one such planet would occur anywhere in the universe" (p. 198).

Scientists often marvel at the beauty, simplicity, rationality, orderliness, and elegance of physical laws. Indeed, this observation has become a pragmatic test for the reasonableness of scientific theories. The more simple and elegant a theory is, the more likely it is to be true. A widely used rule of thumb is Ockham's razor: Choose the simplest theory that explains all the data, cutting away any unnecessary assumptions.

Paul Davies, professor of mathematical physics, stated, "The universe looks *as if* it is unfolding according to some plan or blueprint. . . . Something of *value* emerges as the result of processing according to some ingenious pre-existing set of rules. These rules look *as if* they are the product of intelligent design. I do not see how that can be denied. Whether you wish to believe that they really *have* been so designed, and if so by what sort of being, must remain a matter of personal taste. My own inclination is to suppose that qualities such as ingenuity, economy, beauty, and so on have a genuine transcendent reality—they are not merely the product of human experience—and that these qualities are reflected in the structure of the natural world" (p. 214).

The Anthropic Principle

Some people have sought to evade the overwhelming evidence for divine design by appealing to the "anthropic principle." ("Anthropic" means "relating to humans.") In its weak form it says, "If the universe did not have the

properties it does, we would not be here to observe it."
This is a truism that explains nothing but concedes that
the incredibly improbable occurred. As an analogy, if
someone won the lottery ten times in a row, at the odds of
one in a million each time, we would not say, "It must be
legitimate, because it happened." We would conclude
that this result was due to human intervention—intelligent design, not chance.

Consequently, some people have stated the anthropic
principle in a strong form: "Only a universe that is capable of producing observers can exist." This is an amazing
philosophical view, not a scientific one, for it mystically
credits humans for their own existence. Richard Morris
summarized the alternatives as follows: "Either the universe was designed by a Creator to be hospitable to life,
or the observers that the universe evolves are somehow
responsible for having brought it into existence" (p.
218). In short, the strong anthropic principle puts
humans in the place of God!

Multiple Universes?

Recognizing the inadequacy of the anthropic principle, some agnostics have proposed that there are actually
multiple universes, or the multiverse theory. In this way
they hope to explain the unimaginably small probability
that our fine-tuned universe could have arisen randomly.
To illustrate, suppose the probability of being struck by
lightning is one in a million. This probability is so small
that ordinarily we would not worry about it. Yet since
there are over six billion people on the earth, it is almost
inevitable that someone somewhere will be stricken by
lightning. In the same way, if there are many trillions of

universes, then it becomes more likely that one of them could sustain intelligent life.

Again, this argument is philosophical, not scientific, for by definition we cannot obtain scientific information about anything outside our universe. (If we could, it would be part of our universe.) When people seek some kind of scientific justification for multiple universes, they usually turn to quantum theory. They speculate that its probability distributions represent various realities in parallel universes. But this idea leads to strange paradoxes, resulting not only in multiple copies of particles but also multiple copies of ourselves in other universes. Such theories undermine fundamental concepts of personal existence and free will.

The multiverse theory is a wildly speculative attempt to avoid the obvious. Discarding Ockham's razor, it rejects the simple explanation that an intelligent God created the universe in favor of an extremely complex theory that requires the existence of more universes than all the subatomic particles in our universe. Moreover, it does not answer the fundamental question of origins but shifts it back one level: How and why did these multiplied trillions of universes come into existence? Did God create them, did they create themselves, or have they always existed? We are left with our original question and no answer.

Conclusion

There is overwhelming scientific evidence that the universe was created by an intelligent Designer. The alternate explanations—the anthropic principle and the multiverse theory—are not scientific but are philosophical attempts to avoid belief in God. They assume that the universe somehow created itself but do not offer a mechanism by which it could have done so. Belief in God as the Creator of the universe is still the most reasonable option of all, especially when we experience His creative power in our own lives.

Sources

Davies, Paul. *The Mind of God*. New York: Touchstone, 1992.

Feynman, Richard. *QED: The Strange Theory of Light and Matter*. Princeton, N.J.: Princeton University Press, 1985. (Quantum electrodynamics.)

Hawking, Stephen. *A Brief History of Time*. New York: Bantam, 1988.

Morris, Richard. *The Edges of Science*. New York: Prentice Hall, 1990.

Penrose, Roger. *The Emperor's New Mind*. New York: Oxford University Press, 1989.

Rees, Martin. *Just Six Numbers*. New York: Basic, 2000.

Ross, Hugh. *The Creator and the Cosmos*, 3d ed. Colorado Springs: NavPress, 2001.

Strobel, Lee. *The Case for a Creator*. Grand Rapids: Zondervan, 2004. (Best treatment for a general audience.)

Forward, March-April 2006